The good

- Micro steps -
- Credit cards.
- PO system

ACTIVITY: Identify Sources of Relational Purpose

Instructions:
1. Allocate 100 points across the sources of relational purpose to indi
2. Star the sources of relational purpose where you would like to stre
3. Identify an activity that could help you to close the gaps by making

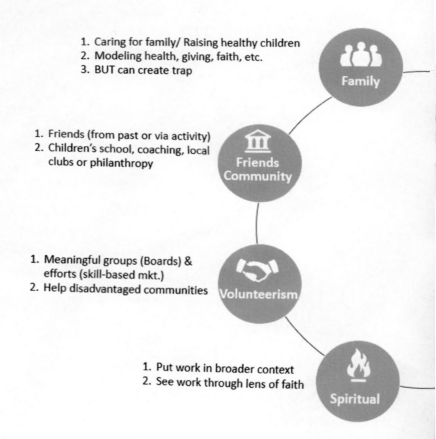

1. Caring for family/ Raising healthy children
2. Modeling health, giving, faith, etc.
3. BUT can create trap

Family

1. Friends (from past or via activity)
2. Children's school, coaching, local clubs or philanthropy

Friends Community

1. Meaningful groups (Boards) & efforts (skill-based mkt.)
2. Help disadvantaged communities

Volunteerism

1. Put work in broader context
2. See work through lens of faith

Spiritual

ater resiliency.

his role for you. Start by thinking about those in your closest group
your broader Community.

		Relational (12-15)	Community (50-150)

STEP 2

fect App
rt
improving

...n you. Place an "X" in the appropriate cells to identify the source(s) of each. *for others.* Place an "O" in these cells.

Who is driving your stress?					
Boss	Leaders	Peers	Client	Team	Loved Ones
				✓	
					X
		X			
					X
	✓				O
				X	O ✓

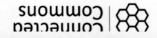

where you are investing energy.
en and invest more energy.
ll shifts.

Culture Leaders

1. **What**: Meaningful mission/ work/company
2. **How**: Holistic organization impact, doing right thing & care for colleague success

Peers

1. Co-create/cascade meaningful future
2. Engage those with similar values
3. Authentic connection with peers

Team Mentor

1. Mentor - helping, seeing growth, sharing your learning, being authentic
2. Create context for team to thrive in work

Consumer

1. Validation from consumers of output
2. Contributing to success of end user (Science curing people; Software enabling orgs)

"*The Microstress Effect* is a revelation. Cross and Dillon offer practical and sensible strategies for regaining control of your time and your well-being, drawn from years of academic research. If small hassles and burdens are infecting your life, this remarkable book is the antidote."

—**DANIEL H. PINK**, #1 *New York Times* bestselling author,
   The Power of Regret, Drive, and *When*

"Cross and Dillon provide fresh insight into one of the most important topics of our time—why so many high performers are at risk of burnout in both their careers and their lives. Based on solid academic research, *The Microstress Effect* offers not only hope but also practical guidance for fending off microstress and living a rich, fulfilling life."

—**SUSAN DAVID**, #1 *Wall Street Journal* bestselling author,
   Emotional Agility

"With stories that everyone can relate to, easy-to-use self-assessments, and practical coaching breaks, the authors offer us real hope that we can create a happier and healthier life for ourselves and those around us. This book should be required reading for corporate leaders and individuals alike! I will be giving it to the people I care most about."

—**JACQUELINE WILLIAMS-ROLL**, Chief Human Resources Officer,
   General Mills

"I read this brilliant book and said "Yup, yup, yup" over and over again. Cross and Dillon put the experiences of high performers into words. Microstresses exist and cause inordinate social, emotional, and physical risk. Following their astute insights, readers will recognize their stresses and how to overcome them. Nothing could be more meaningful in this emotionally demanding time."

—**DAVE ULRICH**, Rensis Likert Collegiate Professor of Business
   Administration, Ross School of Business, University of Michigan;
   Partner, The RBL Group

"Timely, practical, credible, and timeless, with more practical tips for lowering my stress levels than anything I've read in years, *The*

Microstress Effect is a game changer. I read it in one sitting and need the people around me to read it—now!"

—**TOM RATH**, bestselling author, *StrengthsFinder 2.0* and *Life's Great Question*

"Cross and Dillon shed light on the unexpected ripple effect of our daily interactions and relationships, clarifying the critical nature of human connections in this important new book. Introducing microstress as new form of stress, they also provide practical steps for fighting back. Everyone can benefit from reading this book."

—**AMY EDMONDSON**, Novartis Professor of Leadership and Management, Harvard Business School; author, *The Fearless Organization*

"*The Microstress Effect* gives fresh, actionable advice to fight back, take control, and live a richer life each day."

—**DORIE CLARK**, *Wall Street Journal* bestselling author, *The Long Game*; faculty member, Executive Education, Duke University Fuqua School of Business

"With so much attention being paid to individual well-being, it's astounding that so little consideration has been given to the day-to-day microstress every one of us endures. Thank goodness for Rob Cross and Karen Dillon. In *The Microstress Effect* they help us recognize this invisible epidemic and leverage research to help us remove microstress so we can live healthier and happier lives."

—**KEVIN OAKES**, CEO, Institute for Corporate Productivity (i4cp)

"This is an enlightening work on a new, insidious, and invisible form of stress that is derailing even the most high-performing employees. But the authors offer solutions as well. This book should be required reading for business leaders in organizations of all sizes."

—**JOHN BOUDREAU**, Emeritus Professor of Management and Organization, Emeritus, and Research Director, Center for Effective Organizations, Marshall School of Business, University of Southern California

"Cross and Dillon have done a masterful job of flipping our thinking. Their identification of microstressors that sits below our perceptual threshold is uniquely powerful. Just as powerful is the idea that the sheer number of necessary connections we must have today can be reframed and redirected to create resilience rather than spiraling down into collaborative and connective overload. A postpandemic must-read for business leaders."

—**DENNIS BALTZLEY**, Senior Partner and Global Head of
   Leadership Development, Korn Ferry

"*The Microstress Effect* makes a compelling case that, for most of us, it's the cumulative impact of one little problem after another that can ruin our lives. Rob Cross and Karen Dillon pack this lively gem with practical and proven solutions. It will help you eliminate pesky microstressors, suffer less from your remaining troubles, and—by taking joy in the lovely little moments—travel through your days with a zest for life."

—**ROBERT I. SUTTON**, Professor of Organizational Behavior,
   Stanford Graduate School of Business; bestselling author,
   The No Asshole Rule, Good Boss, Bad Boss; and coauthor
   (with Huggy Rao), *Scaling Up Excellence*

"Powerful! *The Microstress Effect* gives you the actionable steps you need to take control of your life and create a balance in your work that leaves you feeling fulfilled. A must-read for anyone feeling stuck in a cycle of stress and hurry!"

—**MARSHALL GOLDSMITH**, Thinkers50 #1 Executive Coach;
   New York Times bestselling author (with Mark Reiter),
   The Earned Life, Triggers, and *What Got You Here
   Won't Get You There*

"Chock full of practical tools, this empowering guide reminds us of the critical importance of relationships and shows us how to meaningfully cultivate them in our everyday choices."

—**STEW FRIEDMAN**, Practice Professor of Management, Emeritus,
   The Wharton School of Business; author, *Total Leadership*

"*The Microstress Effect* is a real eye-opener and will forever change the way I look at stress. I absolutely recommend it for anyone who wants to regain their energy, focus on what truly matters, and live a life fully in alignment with their core values."

—**FRIEDERIKE FABRITIUS**, *Wall Street Journal* bestselling author, *The Brain-Friendly Workplace*

THE
MICROSTRESS
EFFECT

THE
MICROSTRESS
EFFECT

How Little Things Pile Up
and Create Big Problems—
and What to Do about It

ROB CROSS | KAREN DILLON

Harvard Business Review Press
Boston, Massachusetts

Printed in the United Kiigdom by TJ Books Limited, Padstow, Cornwall

10 9 8 7 6 5 4 3 2

Library of Congress Cataloging-in-Publication Data

Names: Cross, Robert L., 1967- author. | Dillon, Karen (Editor), author.
Title: The microstress effect : how little things pile up and create big
    problems--and what to do about it / Rob Cross and Karen Dillon.
Description: Boston, Massachusetts : Harvard Business Review Press, [2023]
    | Includes index. |
Identifiers: LCCN 2022045080 (print) | LCCN 2022045081 (ebook) |
    ISBN 9781647823979 (hardcover) | ISBN 9781647823986 (epub)
Subjects: LCSH: Stress (Psychology) | Job stress. | Resilience (Personality trait) |
    Adjustment (Psychology) | Work-life balance. | Personality and occupation.
Classification: LCC BF575.S75 .C757 2023 (print) | LCC BF575.S75 (ebook) |
    DDC 155.9/042--dc23/eng/20221213
LC record available at https://lccn.loc.gov/2022045080
LC ebook record available at https://lccn.loc.gov/2022045081

ISBN: 978-1-64782-397-9
eISBN: 978-1-64782-398-6

The paper used in this publication meets the requirements of the American National Standard for Permanence of Paper for Publications and Documents in Libraries and Archives Z39.48-1992.

*To our kids: Rachel and Connor and Rebecca and Emma,
who are a constant source of joy and a continual
reminder of the importance of being truly present
with the people we care most about.*

CONTENTS

Invisible and Relentless

W e didn't set out to write this book. For the past two decades, I (Rob Cross) have been studying the underlying network dynamics of effective organizations and the collaborative practices of high performers. I've written extensively about how certain people can work far more productively than others because of how they tap their network of connections. I've tried to identify the flawed assumptions that are often baked into the corporate understanding of who their most valuable employees are and how these people leverage networks to produce results.

But in doing a series of interviews with high achievers about the practices that allow them to be effective collaborators, I stumbled onto something bigger. In one of my first interviews, I heard a wonderful story about the role that connections with others played in helping a life sciences executive shift to a healthier lifestyle after a stern warning from her doctor. She went from being a self-described sedentary workaholic to a person who actively chose vacation destinations where she and her husband could run marathons together. When we spoke, her energy was off the charts, and she was clearly in a great place in her life. Because my interviews were focused on people who had been identified as high performers by their organizations, it made sense that I'd speak with a marathon runner or two. But as she was enthusiastically sharing her new lifestyle with me, I wondered something different. How had someone who was clearly goal-driven neglected her own well-being so drastically? On a whim I asked her what had thrown her so off track in the first place. For a moment, she was stumped. "It was just life, I guess," she told me.

So, we made a point of asking similar questions of the other high performers (three hundred in total, split across women and men) that we interviewed. Many of them were powder kegs of stress. But most of them didn't recognize the state they were in. We would be deep into our interview before they began to acknowledge that they were struggling to keep up with both work and their personal lives. And these people had been identified by their organizations as exceptionally effective performers. During our interviews, many choked up or even broke down into tears, lamenting that they couldn't see a path out of feeling like they were barely holding it all together. After decades of research, I was familiar with the kind of recognizable stress that high performers often endure to achieve their professional goals. But this was something completely different. It was stress but in a form that neither they—nor we—had the language to articulate. What became clear as we talked is that it was never one big thing that led people to feel overwhelmed. Rather, the relentless accumulation of unnoticed small stresses in passing moments is what was drastically affecting the well-being of these people who otherwise appeared to have it all. We call these small pressures *microstress*.

Ample data tells us that people across the world are under unprecedented levels of stress. For example, in its annual State of the Workplace survey, Gallup concluded that only 33 percent of those surveyed were "thriving", with 44 percent of employees reporting experiencing "a lot" of stress in a typical workday—a record high.[1] But little recognized or adequately studied is the toll of this new form of stress. The toll is so subtle that we barely register it, but the cumulative effect can derail even high performers both personally and professionally.

Where is all this microstress coming from?

We all accept that we now live in a hyperconnected 24-7 world, with everyone a simple text, call, or video chat away—in every realm of our lives. We have to be on call to people in both our personal and our professional lives around the clock. But what high performers and other smart people like you, the reader, fail to recognize is how these connections trigger an avalanche of microstress that extends far beyond a lengthy to-do list or full calendar. Because microstress comes from the people we are closest to, personally and professionally, there are layers of emotional complications, too. We can't simply shake it off at the end of the day. Microstress seeps into our thoughts, saps our energy, and diverts our focus. Little by little, it's stealing our lives.

As the heartbreaking stories of many people's lives unfolded in our interviews, I decided to pivot my own work to address this unrecognized epidemic of microstress. As I listened to the high performers discuss the small stresses that had somehow snowballed into pressure affecting their personal well-being, I realized that I, too, was not immune from microstress. Like many of you, I am prone to saying yes to too many projects and requests, assuming I can put my head down and get through any rough patches with a bit of willpower. I had been telling myself I could survive if I could *just get through this one week*. Except every week became that one week. I maintained that philosophy for months on end without a break. And what I hadn't recognized until then was the enduring ripple effects of microstress. I was in the worst shape of my life, and it had been far too long since I'd been truly present with some of the most important people in my life. For personal and professional reasons, I needed to make sense of this phenomenon.

With this sense of urgency in mind, I reached out to Karen Dillon, a former editor of *Harvard Business Review* and coauthor of the *New York Times* bestseller *How Will You Measure Your Life?* to ask if she would collaborate with me on this new work. I'd long been a fan of Karen's work with Harvard Business School professor Clayton Christensen; the work has focused on helping people understand how to live lives of purpose. After being on a fast-track career trajectory herself, she had made some important life changes that allowed her to reframe her own priorities. She had taken the extraordinary step of resigning from her position as editor of *Harvard Business Review* at the peak of her career to refocus her life on her family for a few years. Only after she brought her life back in balance did she begin to fully resume her professional activities. We talked for months about my research before we decided that we not only wanted to write this book but also needed to write it to help other people understand what was happening to them. Working together during the pandemic made this goal even clearer to both of us. There is far too much at stake in your physical and mental health to allow microstress to ruin your life.

And as we wrote this book, both of us made a conscious effort to employ some of the tactics we learned in our research to mitigate our own microstress. We'd catch ourselves falling into old habits, sometimes pausing our meetings to remind ourselves how to avoid unintentionally triggering waves of microstress for the other, or we'd make a point of spending a few minutes on every call connecting personally, even if we were pressed for time. And throughout this process, both of us worked hard to stay connected with our friends and family outside of work in ways designed to combat and even preempt the toll of the microstress that we, too, must deal with. Two years after we began this project, we have gotten our own microstress under better control.

How This Book Can Help

In the pages that follow, we'll share the insights we gained from hundreds of interviews and from Rob's long-term work on collaboration. Through our research, we have found that you can structure your life in ways that not only help diminish microstress but also improve your overall well-being. This approach will involve—in fact require—building and strengthening authentic connections with others. These connections will, in turn, add dimensionality to your life and help you mitigate the effects of microstress. It's a virtuous cycle.

In **chapter 1,** we will define microstress, illustrating what it is and how it's quietly ruining your life. Other chapters will help you identify the sources of microstress in your life so that you can diagnose where your problem spots lie and craft strategies for pushing back.

Chapter 2 identifies microstresses that drain your capacity to get things done. Capacity-depleting microstresses leave many of us feeling as if we're failing both at work and in our personal lives. We can barely get through the responsibilities of our day. This chapter offers practical suggestions for pushing back or restructuring some of your interactions to minimize the impact of this form of microstress.

In **chapter 3**, we'll focus on microstresses that deplete your emotional reserves, the internal pool of peace, fortitude, and resilience that helps you focus, prioritize, and manage fear, anger, anxiety, and concern for those you care about. We'll examine where emotionally draining microstresses are coming from and offer guidance on how to prevent them from eating away at your everyday quality of life.

In **chapter 4**, we'll discuss microstresses that challenge your identity and that trigger the uncomfortable feeling that somehow you're not quite the person you really want to be. These microstresses slowly chip away at your motivation and sense of purpose. This chapter will help you see where these microstresses are affecting your life and offer actionable tips for getting back on course.

Chapter 5 describes how to develop a comprehensive plan for address-ing both the primary and the secondary effects of microstresses. A series of exercises helps you craft a realistic plan for getting the microstresses in your own life under control. The best practices laid out for you here come from the people we call the *ten percenters*—the one-out-of-ten interviewees who successfully navigate their microstress while maintain-ing full and satisfying personal and professional lives. Fortunately, you can incorporate some of the best practices of these ten percenters into your own life, with a little work.

Chapter 6 discusses how people are conditioned to think that resil-ience is something they have to dig deep to find inside themselves. We'll show, instead, how connections with others provide seven predictable forms of resilience that help you navigate difficult stretches—if you have built the relationships and know how and when to tap into them.

In **chapter 7**, we will debunk the conventional wisdom that maintain-ing people's physical health is a solitary activity that relies on willpower.

We ask a tough question: If staying healthy is as simple as knowing what to do and being motivated to take action, then why do so many of us fail in our New Year's Eve resolutions just a few weeks in? Because health is intimately intertwined with the people in your networks, we'll demonstrate how connections with others play a critical role in maintaining (or resurrecting) your physical health, far beyond simply having workout buddies.

Finally, in **chapter 8**, we'll explore the power of finding purpose—specifically, the power of finding purpose in everyday interactions—to help you navigate the daily onslaught of microstresses. The ten percenters in our research were not defined by magnificent undertakings but flourished instead by living small moments more richly with others. Chapter 8 shows you how to find purpose in your own life—not in six months or next year, but tomorrow.

We recognize that asking someone whose life is brimming with microstress to take the time to read a book about their problems might seem counterproductive. But we promise you, the payoff will be real. As we explore the concept of microstress in this book, we hope that you can better articulate something you've already been feeling. And then we can help you make changes. In our research, we have seen that even just pushing back on two or three microstresses can make a significant difference in your day-to-day life. Every chapter has coaching breaks and specific practices you can adopt. We have also written this book so that once you understand the concept of microstress, you can focus on the parts that will have the biggest impact on your life.

Microstress is a solvable problem. You have never had more ability to control what you do and with whom you do it. As one interviewee put it, "I just want to reclaim my life!" You can do exactly that. In the chapters that follow, we will show you how.

Chapter 1

A Crisis of Well-Being

Microstress: *tiny moments of stress triggered by people in our personal and professional lives; stresses so routine that we barely register them but whose cumulative toll is debilitating*

 **KEY INSIGHTS**

- **We can't escape microstress,** because the people who are unwittingly causing it are embedded in our personal and professional lives.

- **Microstress comes at us quickly and in small moments;** it doesn't set off the typical fight-or-flight vigilance systems that help us survive other, more noticeable forms of stress. Our bodies experience the cumulative impact of the microstress, but the cause of that stress remains invisible to us.

- **Microstresses can set off a chain reaction** of primary, secondary, and sometimes tertiary consequences that can last for hours or even days, though you may not connect the effects to the original microstress.

- **You can mitigate the impact of microstress.** You can't eliminate microstress (unless you want to move to a desert island or become a recluse!). But you can learn strategies for reducing its volume, depth, and negative effects and for making your connections with people in your personal and professional networks integral to your well-being.

Something was wrong. Was it chest pain? He couldn't quite tell. The feeling was fleeting, as Brian later told us, "but I was convinced I had a heart problem."[1] In a panic, he headed to the emergency room. As a managing director at one of the world's most well-respected investment banks, Brian had prided himself on his intense devotion to staying fit. He was a committed Peloton cyclist; he could tell you his average heart rate, speed, resistance, and power output on any given day. Having recently lost his mentor to a cardiac event, Brian was hyperaware that the feeling in his chest was not normal for a healthy thirty-eight-year-old. When a battery of tests turned up nothing, Brian assumed the pressure in his chest was all in his imagination. "To be honest, I kind of wigged out there for a little bit," he told us.

We met Brian because he had been identified by his company as a high performer. When we first started talking, we understood why his company had suggested him for our research: Brian seemed to have it all. He had a happy and healthy family, he lived in a tony suburb of a major city, and he was on his way professionally to achieving more than he'd ever imagined possible for a kid from a working-class background. He was the personification of cool confidence. But as we asked Brian to walk us through a typical day in his life, a different pattern emerged. "I feel like I'm failing at everything," he confessed. "Both at work and in my personal life. Nobody is getting enough of me."

As we talked about why he was feeling that way, we were not surprised to hear that Brian had pushed himself to the point of a panic attack.

He had become so used to the daily microstresses in his life that he just plowed through them one by one without recognizing that the cumulative effects of those brief moments lingered beyond the original trigger.

For example, Brian couldn't remember the last time he had enjoyed a good night's sleep. "I just can't shut off my mind at night," he told us. "But it's nothing major. It's just a bunch of small things." He listed the things that were already rattling around in his brain that day. He thought he was sharing his to-do list with us. But we heard a list of microstresses:

- He woke up thinking about how two of his colleagues had not yet finished an analysis he needed for a presentation to other managing directors in two days. He started worrying about the work he would have to do to make up for their shortcoming.

- Because his company spanned time zones around the world, he seldom started his day without waking up to a flood of emails sent overnight and bearing troubling news about the financial markets or happenings somewhere else in the company.

- His boss was notorious for sending demanding late-night emails that changed what he had been asking Brian to work on. Key clients often sent similar late-night emails. His boss and clients seldom acknowledged that their demands represented a change from their original requests. But these shifts not only impacted Brian but also affected all the people he was coordinating with to get the work done.

And that was just the start of his day. Throughout his workday, he was bombarded with microstresses. The day we spoke to him, he told us how he was gearing up to fight for bonuses for his team. Last year, he had lost an internal political battle with another department head for some of the discretionary bonus pool. He was still getting to know his current team because senior leaders in the company kept rotating star players off his work groups to respond to pressing needs in other parts of the company. He didn't want to let his team down this year. As we were finishing our interview, Brian was rushing off to sit down with a senior leader who was increasing pressure on him to raise the firm's profile in capital markets but who didn't seem to understand some of the fundamental challenges of Brian's business unit.

During the brief window of our interview, we could hear his phone and laptop pinging with messages and alerts. "Between email, Slack, and video calls, I'm never off the clock," he told us. "But I have no right to complain. I am financially secure and have a wonderful, supportive spouse and a home that is nicer than I ever thought I would have, and my kids seem to be thriving. What do I have to complain about?"

Microstress isn't just shorthand for having a long to-do list; it's also emotional baggage that's not easy to resolve. The source of microstress is seldom a classic antagonist, such as a spectacularly demanding client or jerk boss. Rather, it comes from the people with whom we are closest: our friends, family, and colleagues. When we first talked, Brian didn't even think to mention a host of other microstresses that were part of his daily personal life, such as his concern for his eighty-five-year-old father, who had told him that he was "experimenting" with the dosages of his medication to see how he felt. His dad consequently sometimes forgot to take his medication altogether, often sleeping through much of the day as a result. With too much daytime sleep, his father couldn't sleep at night and was falling more frequently as he padded around his home in the dark. So, Brian and his wife took turns dropping by his parents' house to check in on them. But this routine was getting harder to do because work was so consuming. Brian's wife had a demanding job, too, and she was up for partnership this year. They probably needed to hire a caregiver, but when would they find time to do that, and would his parents be receptive to it? How would that conversation go?

As Brian's situation demonstrated, emotional baggage is the guilt we harbor, the sense that we've let down a loved one, or the concern we feel for their well-being. The emotion in the relationship—positive or negative—magnifies the impact of the stressor. Microstresses may be tiny, but they're complicated. Table 1-1 details how microstress differs from the routine stresses we've come to accept as part of our lives.

TABLE 1-1

How stress differs from microstress

Stress: Coping with a mercurial boss whose daily mood permeates the entire office.

Microstress: The moment your well-intended boss shifts your priorities, yet again.

Secondary microstresses: The moment you call your team to regroup because the work you've all been killing yourselves to get done is no longer a priority and you have to realign. Again.

Stress: Getting diagnosed with stage 2 cancer.

Microstress: The moment you realize you have no chance of making your weekly tennis match with friends and the sinking feeling that your fitness is slipping away from you.

Secondary microstresses: The moment you deliver the bad news to your friends that, once again, you can't make it. You can tell that they're getting annoyed with you. You worry that they'll kick you out of the tennis group—and that you'll not only lose your workout but also lose your regular connection with these people.

Stress: Realizing that your aging parents can no longer live on their own and having to rearrange your life to help them.

Microstress: The moment you try to schedule family calls about caring for your aging parents when you have siblings in different time zones.

Secondary microstresses: The moment you brief your spouse on the latest passive-aggressive conversation with your siblings about your different perspectives on what your parents need and your spouse further fuels your irritation by pointing out that your siblings don't appreciate you enough. Emotionally caught up in all the back-and-forth with your siblings, you eat up time on a Sunday that you had planned to spend with your children.

Stress: Dealing with a child who is struggling with a serious eating disorder.

Microstress: The moment you look down at your phone and see a vaguely worrying text from your teen—"I was the only one not invited to Richard's party"—when you're in a meeting.

Secondary microstresses: The moment you stop focusing on work, so you can spend the rest of the afternoon surreptitiously monitoring your child's social media to try to pick up any clues about what's going on.

Stress: Facing a high-pressure ultimatum from your boss, who says that if your department doesn't meet challenging sales goals, you'll be fired.

Microstress: The moment your boss announces that your company is updating its standard contract with longtime customers to require faster payments and you will have to be the bearer of that bad news to clients you know will have a hard time complying with the new terms.

Secondary microstresses: The moment you ruminate over how you can deliver this news without damaging the relationships you've worked so hard to build. This anxiety preoccupies you so much you don't get around to making customer calls, because you're worried about doing it wrong.

(continued)

TABLE 1-1

Stress: Surviving multiple rounds of layoffs that eliminated positions in your department.

Microstress: The moment you realize that two teammates have fallen short on their part of your joint project and you're going to have to put in extra time to finish it.

Secondary microstresses: The moment you realize you're going to have to put aside the growth project you're excited about, because you have to focus on cleaning up your colleagues' underdelivery. You also worry about the possibility of having an uncomfortable conversation with them after the deadline to talk about their shortcomings.

Stress: Navigating a contentious divorce that's not only dividing your family but also depleting your savings.

Microstress: The moment you call your spouse to say you won't be home in time to make your daughter's softball game, even though you'd promised you would.

Secondary microstresses: The moment you have to ask your spouse to deliver the bad news to your daughter, causing both your spouse and your daughter to subtly take out their frustration on you for the rest of the week.

Table 1-2 summarizes the fourteen common microstresses according to three categories that are the focus of this book. In later chapters, we will look at each of these microstresses in depth.

We suspect that as you scanned the list, you could immediately tick off at least a few microstresses that you're dealing with. By our count, Brian was experiencing almost all fourteen microstresses. And that was just on one particular day. Though there might be variations on the same themes, many of us would probably describe our daily lives in similar ways. And like Brian, you might assume that you just have to accept microstresses as the way things are.

Each of these individual moments in the microstress column may seem manageable. After all, they are mere moments. But we often fail to see how microstresses set off a chain reaction of primary, secondary, and sometimes even tertiary consequences that can last for hours or days, invading your life in ways that you don't connect to the original stress. Microstresses can cause a myriad of problems, including these:

- **They deplete your time.** When you have to invest too much time working toward and resolving an issue, you cut into the time you need for other work obligations. This loss of time creates stress as

TABLE 1-2

Fourteen common microstresses, by category

Capacity-draining microstresses	Emotion-depleting microstresses	Identity-challenging microstresses
Misaligned roles and priorities	Managing and advocating for others	Conflict with your personal values
Small performance misses from colleagues	Confrontational conversations	Interactions that undermine confidence
Unpredictable authority figures	Lack of trust	Draining or other negative interactions with family or friends
Inefficient communication practices	Secondhand stress	Disruptions to your network
Surges in responsibilities	Political maneuvering	

you worry about your commitments to others, how you will find the time to do that work, and what colleagues' reactions will be if you give short shrift to something or miss a deadline.

- **Microstresses derail you from your own goals.** Being pulled in different directions keeps you in a reactive mode, where you're less able to shape your own work efforts toward things that you personally care about. As a result, you are always busy but are unable to do the things that matter for your own long-term career success and sense of purpose.

- **They make you sacrifice your personal commitments.** The scramble to get work done can cause you to shirk or shortchange personal commitments to family, friends, and other groups to which you belong. Who hasn't dreaded delivering the news that you can't keep a commitment to a loved one? And it's not just the ever-present guilt of missing a child's soccer game or school play. It's also a product of slowly removing activities and relationships outside of your immediate family from your priority list. Making your life smaller to cope with the endless stream of microstress can wreak havoc on your physical and mental health.

- **They drag loved ones into your work stress.** When you are forced to back out of your commitments because of microstresses that tax you at work, you add microstress to your relationships outside work. Or you share your microstress with your loved ones, relaying your version of an injustice that you've had to endure. As supportive spouses and friends tend to do, they empathize and share your outrage. Their feedback feels good for a moment, but in reality, it can loop back on you, magnifying the initial impact of the microstress. *You're right, they are taking advantage of me!* You spiral further into the microstress. And now your loved ones are emotionally involved, too.

- **Microstresses damage relationships in your network.** Many of us resort to calling in personal favors when we're enduring microstress. Perhaps you enlisted a teammate to stay late to conduct an analysis or draft a section of your slide deck for an upcoming presentation. Or you asked a colleague to call in a favor with a vendor. But a sudden shift in expectations from a client or leader changed what you need to get done, making the favor and the stress it caused pointless. "If I would have known that you weren't going to need that data Monday morning, I wouldn't have worked over the weekend."

And of course, you're never coping with just one or two microstresses. Like Brian, you're likely to be facing dozens in a given day. And they pile on, week after week and month after month. So, you're exhausted and burned out, but you can't quite put your finger on why. There's a reason for that.

How Our Brains Respond to Microstress

Microstress is particularly pernicious because it is baked into our everyday lives at a volume, intensity, and pace we have never experienced. And yet our bodies don't quite know what to make of it. The process by which our body normally responds to stresses is called *allostasis*, the biologic mechanisms that protect the body from internal and external stress and help maintain internal homeostasis, or internal balance. Our brains know how to register conventional forms of stress; we identify the threat and use the extra oomph of the fight-or-flight mechanisms that kick in to deal with threats.

Unfortunately, microstresses fly under the radar of these typical vigilance systems, while still taking a significant toll. Joel Salinas, a behavioral neurologist and researcher at the New York University Grossman School of Medicine and chief medical officer at Isaac Health, which provides online brain health services, explained. "Imagine wind eroding a mountain," said Salinas, whose research focuses on the impact of psychosocial factors on brain health. "It's not the same as a big TNT explosion that punches a hole in a mountain. But over time—if the wind never stops—it has the potential to slowly wear an entire mountain down to a nub." We may not be consciously aware of microstresses, but they can increase our blood pressure and our heart rate (as happened during Brian's panic attack) or trigger hormonal or metabolic changes. "So, while microstresses are damaging our bodies, our brains are not registering them fully as a threat," Salinas says. "And therefore, our brains are not triggering the same kind of protective higher-order mechanisms that might occur in the face of more obvious stress."

The brain fails to recognize microstress partly because of how it processes information. The working-memory part of the brain occupies the frontal lobe. Our working memory is where we keep mental notes, a kind of mental scratch pad, Salinas says. But under continual stress, the scratch pad in the frontal lobe tends to shrink; we have a harder time keeping track of things that require our response or attention. This explains why so many of us felt a kind of brain fog during the pandemic. A brain that is inundated with microstresses doesn't have the normal bandwidth to pay attention to an activity or problem-solving. We feel extraordinarily stressed, but we may not remember why. "This is arguably worse than threats that cross the fight-or-flight threshold," Salinas said. "Not only are you not noticing it, but it can also have more severe consequences."

So, while you may be quick to dismiss microstress as something you can deal with, your brain might not. In fact, the human brain doesn't seem to distinguish between different sources of chronic stress, according to neuroscientist Lisa Feldman Barrett, distinguished professor of psychology at Northeastern University and author of *7½ Lessons about the Brain*.[3] The effect of stress, even from "momentary stressors," Barrett writes, is clear. "If your body budget is already depleted by the circumstances of life—like physical illness, financial hardship, hormone surges, or simply not sleeping or exercising enough—your brain becomes more vulnerable to stress of all kinds."

One study found that if you're exposed to social stress within two hours of a meal, your body metabolizes the food in a way that adds 104 calories to what you consumed.[4] "If this happens daily, that's eleven pounds gained per year!" Barrett concludes. "Not only that, but if you eat healthful, unsaturated fats, such as those found in nuts, within one day of being stressed, your body metabolizes these foods as if they were filled with bad fats."

And of course, as microstresses are added to your daily life, they don't land on an empty plate—most of us are already running at full capacity, overtaxed by a baseline of demands across work and personal life. "When your body budget is continually burdened," explains Barrett, "momentary stressors pile up, even the kind that you'd normally bounce back from quickly. It's like children jumping on a bed. The bed might withstand ten kids bouncing at the same time, but the eleventh one snaps the bed frame."

That's what happened to Brian. His life was filled with microstresses jumping on his metaphorical bed. These stresses can cumulatively build in a way that makes you even more vulnerable to any form of stress, however small. It's a vicious cycle.

A Hidden Epidemic

What's become abundantly clear is that we are in an epidemic of microstress. It's ruining lives. The stories people shared with us were often painful. And these were all successful people—they started our sessions with a veneer of positivity about how great things were in life. But after about forty-five minutes, we discovered how deeply even this group of people was struggling. In many of the interviews, people choked up or were in tears at one point or another.

We heard stories of people being on the fast track at work only to feel as if they were actually failing at everything just when they were about to reach one of their goals. "All that work stress was amplified by immediate family stress," one interviewee told us. "Everything just kind of spiraled out of control for a couple years." We heard about strained relationships, people neglecting their physical health, a loss of interest in activities they once loved, dwindling friend groups, a shrinking sense of identity, and so much more. Most of the interviewees just accepted these downsides as an inevitability of modern life.

The old story of the frog in boiling water demonstrates how destructive microstress can be. If you put a frog into a pot of boiling water, the animal will immediately jump out. But if you put a frog in a pot of cool water and slowly increase the heat, the frog adapts and tolerates the heat—until the point where the water gets too hot, and the frog can no longer jump out. Too many of us are sitting in that slowly boiling water because we don't realize what's happening to us. As we heard repeatedly in stories from the people we interviewed, everything was OK. Until it wasn't.

That fate is not inevitable, however. There are ways to navigate this sea of microstress without letting it knock you off course.

Chapter 2

Why You Can't Keep Up Anymore

 **KEY INSIGHTS**

- **Microstresses that drain our personal capacity** sneak into our already-overloaded days, make the days longer and less fulfilling, force us to endure the costs of constantly switching focus, cause us to be less productive, and bleed into our personal lives. Capacity-draining microstresses have five typical causes:

    - Misaligned roles and priorities
    - Small performance misses from colleagues
    - Unpredictable authority figures
    - Inefficient communication practices
    - Surges in responsibilities

- A single microstress that happens in just a moment or two can trigger **ripple effects that last for hours or even days**—not just for you but also for your colleagues, your family, and your friends.

- **You can push back on microstresses that drain personal capacity** in a way that makes a significant difference in your everyday life, once you understand their source and toll they're taking.

A single email from Anthony, the new head of marketing, cata-
pulted Rita, the manager of multiple teams, into a spiral of
panic. Sent off to a half dozen leaders and forwarded down the
chain of command, Anthony's email asked people to create materials for
an upcoming executive presentation. The email seemed urgent but lacked
detail, leaving every recipient with questions. When does he need the
materials? Slides or talking points? Is there a common template? Importantly, what's the story he wants to tell?

In some ways, the email couldn't have been simpler: a routine request
from a leader to a team to prepare for a known presentation. But that
single communication spurred hours of stress throughout the entire organization. Emails flew across the marketing department as Rita and
her colleagues tried to read between the lines. Several recipients had
discussed the presentation with the marketing director in the past few
weeks, but each of those conversations yielded a slightly different version
of what Anthony wanted, confusing things more.

Ninety minutes after receiving Anthony's message, Rita had dealt with
thirty-four emails asking for direction or complaining about the timeline.
In the meantime, two people on the thread had gone ahead and done
what they thought Anthony wanted and forwarded the results to her.
But each of them had used different data sources that told an incompat-
ible story. She didn't discover this discrepancy, however, until 6:30 p.m.,
when she finally had enough time to look at their work after spending the
day firefighting and being yanked from her priorities. By then, of course,
both people had already left for the day. Rita was just one of a handful
of people who were supposed to be working on this project. How had it
become her job to clear up the inconsistency?

Rita had hoped to eat dinner with her teenage son that night. Recently,
he'd become sullen and was spending more time than normal in his room.
Maybe she was imagining it, but she was eager to find time to talk to
him. Unfortunately, she didn't feel she could leave until she had at least
reached out to her colleagues to try to clear up the data question. By the
time she finally drove out of the parking lot, she knew her son would
likely have scavenged food from the fridge and retreated to his room

for the night. Yet again, she'd missed a window to connect with him. The new marketing director might have assumed that his was a simple request—he wanted to see data presented in a couple of ways—but his request had ended up dominating her afternoon and evening. Getting the right data, rerunning the numbers, and putting them into visual presentation mode required several colleagues to drop what they were doing to give Rita what she needed. She set her alarm early so that she could review the materials with fresh eyes in the morning.

Unfortunately, there was nothing particularly unusual about that day for Rita. And the same is probably true for most of us. Any given day can be filled with a range of seemingly small requests or priority shifts that upend our day, causing us to drop what we are doing to focus on something else. We have to put in extra hours at work and push family and friends to the side in the process. Our days are filled with microstresses that drain our personal capacity, decreasing our ability to get things done—at work and in our personal life. When these microstresses hit us, we typically don't pause long enough to register what they're doing to us. We just soldier on. But that doesn't mean they don't take a toll. Microstresses that drain our capacity trigger a chain reaction of other, unrecognized stresses that can stretch for hours, even days. We work harder and longer to compensate, straining our personal relationships in the process. Or we deliver subpar work because we ran out of time, which in turn causes stress in our professional relationships when we underdeliver for people who are counting on us.

Microstresses That Drain Capacity

In the pages that follow, we will define and explore the five categories of capacity-draining microstresses and explain how they creep into your everyday life. From our research, we will share case studies of how some people were affected by these microstresses. And finally, we'll offer practical suggestions to help you push back on this form of microstress.

The point of Rita's story is not that she couldn't handle a last-minute request from the marketing manager. The point is that there is no such

FIGURE 2-1

The ripple effects of one capacity-draining microstressor

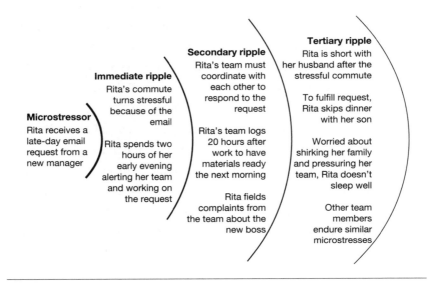

thing as a microstress in isolation. Microstresses always trigger more microstress. When you add up the cumulative toll on Rita and her colleagues and family, you can see the long-reaching tentacles of that one microstress (figure 2-1).

Let's examine more closely the sources of microstress that are draining your personal capacity.

Microstress 1: Misaligned Roles and Priorities

Most people have experienced the frustration of being on teams whose members are pursuing slightly different priorities and that struggle to unite under a common vision or deliver integrated work efficiently. As we move into more agile ways of working and find ourselves on not one cross-functional team but many, the inefficiencies multiply. One of the most common pain points the people we interviewed experienced was being part of teams that didn't recognize or address misalignment until late in a project. No one creates this misunderstanding intentionally; teammates leave meetings assuming everyone is clear on what needs to happen. But throughout our research, we have heard hundreds of stories of projects that became major headaches—and some that delayed or even derailed careers—that at their root came down to *small misalignments not addressed early.*

Misalignments happen in predictable ways, often when people simply attack a problem or an assignment from their own perspective without ever stopping to clarify how their work fits into the bigger picture. Here are three common ways that priorities are misaligned:

- **Different objectives:** This misalignment often arises because team members have different functional priorities. Let's say your team consists of people from marketing, IT, and product development. Even though you all agree on the deadline for launch, each of you might have very different objectives for the six weeks leading up to it, depending on how your performance is measured and rewarded. Every goal is essential to the product launch, but you're all looking at the deliverables from a slightly different point of view. In theory, your leader and your colleague from another department have the same deliverable on a joint project, but each of them might be determined to flex their own unique political muscle, nudging the team in various directions and confusing everyone.

- **Different values:** People's unique expertise, responsibilities, or passions lead them to consider some aspects of their work as the most important. This has less to do with how work is evaluated and rewarded and more to do with what people feel is innately right in the work. One person might prioritize technical excellence and spend disproportionate time modeling and troubleshooting engineering issues at the expense of a more elegant design that would appeal to customers. Another might prize customer feedback and push the project to meet customer demands rather than the most technically efficient engineering solutions. This misalignment can lead to frustration from all sides during routine project meetings.

- **Unclear requirements:** Poor project management leaves well-intended teammates unclear on deliverables, and this lack of clarity triggers microstress. Without clear direction, teammates fill in the blanks on their own, often pursuing the wrong objectives or wasting their time on work that others deem unnecessary. This unfocused approach creates additional downstream microstress, as people need to have side conversations and rejigger their workflows to get the clarity they need.

There are a few quick ways to check for misalignment. Try asking team members what success looks like for a given project. If everyone has a slightly different answer, you may have spotted the source of microstress. Or if you notice that meetings routinely run long but still end up feeling unproductive, you may not all be on the same page. (One telling sign is people's tendency to scramble to get to their next meeting without allowing time for a quick wrap-up or review of what you just agreed to.) Or if you find yourself not feeling proud of the collective team's output, you may be seeing a project where everyone thought they were doing the right thing but where none of you were aligned and the results show it.

Misalignment, of course, has knock-on effects. Take Mark, a recently promoted operations manager in a business services organization, who couldn't understand why he was receiving increasingly negative feedback. The promotion meant that he was now reporting to leaders in two business units, a welcome increase in both his responsibility and visibility in the organization. He was now leading a team responsible for rapid fixes to crucial software problems that impacted large customers. Three team leaders with different responsibilities reported up to him. Conceptually, the new position was a good fit for Mark, who was known for both his problem-solving skills and getting things done.

But since the promotion, Mark felt that he couldn't do anything right. He found himself playing Whac-A-Mole with customer complaints. He was working longer hours, including nights and weekends, to try to get on top of the work. At a time when Mark should have been building morale and establishing his credibility as a leader, his new team was doubting whether he was up to the job.

Worse, he was taking his frustration home at night. When he announced that he might not have the time to attend his wife's long-planned college reunion, she was annoyed. "You've known this was important to me for months," she told him. "Why didn't you plan better?"

Mark was kicking himself daily for not being on top of the job. But what Mark didn't recognize—at first—was that the sources of all his microstress were a series of small misalignments.

It turned out that each of his key team leads had a slightly different perspective on what constituted the resolution to a problem. For the quality team, resolution meant identifying the root cause; for the engineering team, resolution meant a technical solution. The product management team saw resolution as the final rollout of the fix to customers. Clients, on the other hand, expected all three resolutions to happen at the same time. Without a shared model of success, the hand-offs between teams were often clumsy, inefficient, and poorly timed. And Mark realized that he, too, had never clarified his own expectations with any of the teams, leaving them to draw their own conclusions about what success looked like.

To get realigned, he scheduled separate meetings with each of the two leaders he reported to and then one meeting with both those leaders and Mark's full team to get everyone on the same page about what resolution meant. Every person on the team had honestly believed they were doing what was asked of them, but they hadn't recognized how their narrow perspective might have created problems for the team as a whole. It was an eye-opening exercise for everyone, including Mark's two new managers. The result was a single prioritized set of expectations for Mark's unit, additional resources for hiring more people to handle these priorities, and an escalation path for problems that were deemed out of scope. Within a few months of working this way, Mark regained his confidence—and his reputation for being a great project manager.

COACHING BREAK

Fixing the Microstress of a Misaligned Team

If you sense that your team is not aligned, you need to get on top of the problem quickly. Follow this process to course correct misalignments before they trigger more microstress for everyone.

Gather your team for a quick alignment meeting. "I suspect that we are each interpreting the goal of the project slightly differently. Can we take thirty minutes in the next couple of days to make sure we're aligned?" In the meeting, focus on how the misalignment is affecting team members. If you can make clear to everyone how inefficient and frustrating the misalignment is, the team should be open to course correcting. Take the following sequence of steps to correct your course:

1. **Reestablish the purpose or importance of the project in a collaborative discussion.** Focus on the impact that can be generated if the group works together. Appeal to higher-order goals that engage everyone—such as the way the new software will democratize work for customers or how the research will help create more affordable medications. Make sure people can see how they contribute to these goals. The meeting should not open with discussions of timelines and past misses. Rather, start with aspirations of what can be done, and then move on to getting concrete commitments from people and clarity on obstacles that need to be removed.

2. **Talk through how each person's (or team's) work is contributing to the overall project.** Identify the resources needed for each person's or team's work. Make sure everyone is clear on what they are being asked to do—and what they are assuming others will do.

3. **Have a candid discussion on obstacles that would keep people from executing.** This conversation might take the form of reviewing available time, resources, or pressure from a team member's

functional leader to prioritize other work. Some obstacles you will be able to resolve (e.g., speaking with a team member's leader). And some you won't (e.g., resources). But identifying the impediments allows you to create timelines and assignments that are more realistic and an escalation path for problems that are out of scope.

4. **Sketch out visually the interdependencies so they are clear.** Visually capture the interdependencies that will affect others' work. The sketch doesn't need to be a perfect flowchart; a rough road map for the entire team is sufficient. Leave the whiteboard (physical or virtual) up for every meeting. There are many virtual tools for this collaborative task (e.g., Miro and Notion allow you to create a shared whiteboard with sticky notes that everyone can modify).

5. **Secure commitments from each team member regarding work they are doing.** Use the final few minutes of the meeting to have everyone repeat their expectations and the actions they will take before the next meeting. Agree to open each new meeting (whether in person or virtually) with a review of the whiteboard as a visual reminder of where you were and where you're going and to identify any new or brewing misalignments.

STRATEGIES TO AVOID MISALIGNMENT MICROSTRESS. You can take several practical steps to avoid having small misalignments creep into your work. They depend on your willingness to pause and ask questions at various junctures of the work to ensure that a small misalignment is corrected before it spirals into something bigger.

Before a New Project, Investigate Relational Complexity

One of the hidden sources of microstress lies with the increased collaborative footprint of work today. The number and kinds of collaborations we need to engage in to do our work has exploded but we often don't factor this time into our estimates of how much time a task or project will require.

- **Consider relationships and contingencies.** Think through the web of relationships and contingencies that would be involved in a new task or project, including how they would interact with what's currently on your or your team's plate. Who will you depend on to get this task done? Will they work together seamlessly, or is the collaborative footprint required to get the work done larger than anticipated?

- **Review the goals, priorities, and stakeholders.** Speak with the project sponsor and leader to make sure you clearly understand the goals, priorities, and stakeholders involved. It can be tempting to say yes to new projects because you want to help the person asking you or to convey a can-do attitude, but you can be open and positive while saying "I'd like to learn more" before committing.

- **Clarify the magnitude of the request.** Talk with everyone involved, including people on other projects you work with, to ensure that they understand what is involved in the new project and that it's doable for you, considering your competing priorities.

When Starting a New Project, Clarify What You Are Committing To

- **Agree to what and when.** Early on, take the time with the team to ensure that you agree on the what and when of the work. Take five minutes to clarify specifics for yourself, your stakeholders, and any other colleagues contributing to the effort.

- **Clarify what you are accountable for.** You must understand the magnitude of the request to know whether you—and the colleagues you'll be relying on—have the time and the capability required to accomplish the work.

- **Lay out a clear timeline, along with performance expectations.** A shared understanding at the outset is critical to everyone's success.

While Working Together, Be Vigilant for Misalignments

- **Develop your own sensor system for uncovering misalignments so that you can engage quickly to fix problems.** Consider using the last five or ten minutes of a meeting to ask people to repeat what they're taking away from a conversation, to make sure there are no misinterpretations.

- **Pay attention to your intuition.** An uncomfortable feeling that arises after a meeting might be a sign that everyone is not on board.

- **Consider writing a follow-up email.** Even something as simple as a brief bullet-pointed recap of key assumptions can ensure that the team agrees on goals, responsibilities, timeframes, and deliverables. Too often we can leave a meeting assuming we're all on the same page, but then spin off in different directions unintentionally.

Microstress 2: Small Performance Misses

Another significant source of microstress comes from colleagues who are unreliable, but not in the way you might think. It's not so much the slackers who hurt us, as they're often weeded out by performance management and talent processes in organizations. More often than not, problems arise when minor missteps in performance from well-intended teammates add up in surprising ways. Most of us are pulled in so many directions that we forget, fall behind, or hope that "good enough" will suffice, because we are overwhelmed with responsibilities. We cut corners, none of them seemingly significant, in ways that end up affecting not just our own work but that of our colleagues as well.

Imagine you're in charge of a project with three other team members. One person didn't fully understand the commitment required, a second got pulled into another priority project and put in less time than was anticipated, while a third prioritized a looming deadline for a sales meeting and gave your project short shrift. Under those circumstances, each of those people might miss the mark on your project by just a bit, say, falling 5 percent short of expectations. The slipups might take the form of a delay in gathering data that the rest of the team needs, failing to proofread a draft of a report, overlooking the cross-unit resources needed, and so on.

In isolation, these small misses might seem insignificant. But they are not small to you—or to the project outcome. You feel responsible for the project, or you don't want your own reputation to suffer because of a subpar team effort. You step up—as you almost always do—to make up for what your colleagues fell short on. To compensate for your colleagues, you might need to do 15 percent extra work on a schedule that is already maxed out—not to mention that you have to upend your own workload outside of this project. Many of us would never even complain to our colleagues about the shortcomings, simply charging into heroic effort to save the day.

The microstress here—your colleagues falling just a bit short on what you expected them to do—affects future work as well. Now you not only have to do extra work on top of your own, but you've also trained your colleagues that 95 percent effort is good enough—and maybe 90 percent next time, if they are getting pulled in too many directions. They know that you'll compensate to back them up when they get too busy or distracted. And in some ways, you've done this to yourself by stepping up! The spillover effect from your being inundated with their work on top of yours will also ripple over into your other work, your home life, your relationship with your manager, and so on.

In the best-case scenario, it's disheartening to realize you must pick up the slack for someone else when you're barely keeping up with your own work. In the worst case, you can build up resentment toward people who aren't coming through on their commitments, and your resentment undermines otherwise-solid working relationships. "Somehow I'm always the one cleaning up after my colleagues don't come through," one interviewee told us. "I know they're not doing it intentionally. We're all overstretched. But somehow, it's always me that feels the need to step in."

Kunal, a senior leader in the automotive industry, shared the frustration he felt when a subordinate turned in a substandard work product. "It creates a sort of seething bitterness and stress because I'm now doing something I shouldn't be doing," he told us. "Doing their work displaces other things and contributes to an environment where I don't have the energy and time to develop my team." As a manager, he was responsible for his team's work. But when team members fell short, he found himself not only scrambling to do his employees' work for them but also trying to find time to address the performance issue. The situation adds a whole other layer of microstress to Kunal's day. "That requires extra energy," he said, "because you have to be understanding and then follow almost a Socratic process that walks someone through the preparation they should have done." For Kunal, coping with an underperforming subordinate created new, unplanned work, upending his day and making it harder for him to focus on his own priorities. And that's just the immediate consequences. Over time, the double duty built resentment, caused him to call in favors from other team members, and meant that he often brought his frustration home at night. He was aware that he was bringing his problems home, but he couldn't seem to shake off the day.

Practices to Combat Small Performance Misses

In any fast-paced organization where people are juggling collaborative projects, tight deadlines, and their individual work, performance misses are bound to crop up. But if the misses can be caught and addressed early, you can prevent them from spiraling into something with lasting microstress consequences. Here are some ways to prevent or address microstresses before they create more damage.

CREATE ACCOUNTABILITY. Capture clear descriptions of the work to be done, who is accountable for each objective, and what success looks like. One person in our research used a kanban board (a board that visually depicts work at various stages of a process, using cards to represent work items and columns to represent each stage of the process) to communicate

COACHING BREAK

Addressing Small Performance Misses

Small errors can take many forms. Some slipups affect only you, whereas others might upset an entire team. Some might just have a short-term, limited impact, but others might ripple on. The key is to think about these misses along three dimensions and take the appropriate corrective action.

STAFF IMPACT: Does the Small Miss Affect Me Alone or the Full Team?

- **Me:** Address the shortcoming directly in discussion. Acknowledge that it is a small slip and that addressing it might seem petty. Indicate the impact of the accumulation of small misses and how this buildup is affecting your professional and personal life. Collaboratively problem-solve with a focus on three issues: (1) what you can do differently, (2) what the other person can do differently, and (3) what circumstances need to be changed to make this work (e.g., do you need to speak with the person's leader to secure more time?).

- **Team:** Leverage social pressure in team meetings by having people open the discussion with a restatement of their commitment, a brief on their progress, and a short summary of what's gone wrong and why. Begin meetings with this structured check-in to create a norm of accountability. Close meetings with people recapping commitments to make sure that expectations are consistent. Use a visual tool during the meeting (and post it to team members afterward) to have a clear reference for accountability.

FREQUENCY: Is This the First Time This Slip Has happened, or is It a Recurring Pattern?

- **First time:** Do not be afraid to address small misses early. Too often, people step up to fill a void and, in so doing, become angry.

Unfortunately, they are teaching their colleagues that less than a full effort is acceptable. People sometimes go light on their responsibilities not because they are evil but because all of us are pulled in so many directions that most of us are trying to figure out which balls can be dropped (not how to meet all commitments). Tackle the first slipup early, with a lighthearted comment and an authentic desire to help, and you will keep an initial small miss from becoming malignant.

- **Recurring:** Have a direct conversation on the impact of this recurrence. Then ask how you can help. Lead with what you can do or what changes to the situation may help prevent the same issue from coming up again and again. This helps keep defensiveness from preventing constructive conversation. Then move on to what that person needs to do to ensure the same problems don't recur.

MAGNITUDE: What is the Magnitude of the Miss? Will the Slipup Wash Away in a Week, or Will It Have a Lingering or Large Impact for Some Time?

- **Small or temporary effect:** Start with empathy and consider letting go of your concern. Most people are struggling with a tsunami of personal and professional obligations. More often than not, a miss on your project is not what they wanted to do but is just the reality of too many professional and personal demands in today's hyperconnected world. Not everything will be done well or done at all.

- **Lingering or large effect:** Take the same approach that you would for recurring slips: have a direct conversation with the person on the impact of this recurrence. Then ask how you can help. Lead with what you can do, and make changes to the current situation to help avoid a recurring issue. Then move to what that person must do differently.

and get agreement on expectations, but many other visual tools could also work, depending on the circumstances.

Take a few minutes at the end of team meetings to review whatever visual tool you're using, and ask where everyone is in terms of progress. The goal here is to depersonalize discussions about small misses and place responsibility back on the accountable parties. This practice prevents further slippage and ensures a consistent norm of delivery in the team.

FIND PROBLEMS EARLY. Establish a tempo of check-ins with colleagues to make sure that small oversights become visible as soon as possible. Noticing an execution gap early allows you to find out why it has happened when there may still be time to address the root causes and course-correct in a way that strengthens relationships.

Situations where individuals can't deliver because of outside pressures need a different response from situations where people may lack the necessary capabilities. Outside pressures may require an email or a phone call from you to get others to back down for a bit, whereas people who are in over their heads may need developmental support or help with renegotiating their roles.

CHECK PROGRESS. Set a midpoint reminder to connect with people when half of their work should be completed. Use this check-in as an early opportunity to see how far they've progressed, to look at the state of their work product, and to make sure they're heading in the right direction.

Microstress 3: Unpredictable Authority Figures

Unpredictable behavior from a person in authority, such as a boss, a senior leader, or a client, can create an undercurrent of microstress. We're not talking about dealing with an exceptionally difficult or unreasonable person—such a person is a conventionally recognized source of stress and one you are painfully aware of. Because you probably have allies who see and feel the same way about a problematic person, this kind of stress doesn't feel so personal. What we're talking about here is a common microstress that you don't stop to think about: a well-intentioned boss, client, or stakeholder who seems to constantly be slightly altering what they are asking of you.

Shifting demands or frequently revisiting decisions can throw us off balance or create uncertainty about where to commit our energies. *Is this a priority or that? Am I supposed to drop everything to turn to this new assignment, or was that just a passing comment?* And when you are never quite sure what emotional state your boss will be in, the situation can trigger an enormous amount of stress and concern. *Was she annoyed just then? Is he worried about this getting done? Is my team screwing up in some way that I don't see?* You may overthink what you're doing or produce twice the work you actually need to in attempts to cover all the bases.

And it's not simply that you have to figure out how to handle the demands coming your way from a boss. The struggle also plays out in your relationships with others you work with. You set expectations for people on your team, and you deliver (or don't) according to your understanding of what the boss wants. You communicate with others what you think your boss wants you to communicate. And when that message is hard to figure out, the ambiguity affects your work with a whole host of other people, too. You may be constantly tweaking or completely changing what you're asking other people to do, the favors you're calling in, or the pressure and priorities you place on different projects or deliverables. Perhaps you've had to deliver the bad news to a colleague who has been working overtime to finish a complex analysis or a draft of something that you realize you no longer need. Or you whip your colleagues into a frenzy to get something done and then they are demoralized when shifting priorities from a leader or client makes that work meaningless.

Unpredictability was in part driving Rita's stress from that single email from Anthony, the new head of marketing. Her previous boss had been methodical about routine staff meetings and decision-making. But Anthony was informal and often seemed to shift his priorities, so Rita was always scrambling to keep up. As a result, she frequently had to call in favors or trade help with other colleagues to meet his latest requests.

In a typical encounter, Anthony would send Rita an email with what seemed to be an urgent request—like the one for the presentation discussed at the start of this chapter. Rita would drop what she was doing and try to track down a colleague to compare notes. When she would send her response back to the manager, Rita would rarely receive even a courtesy reply. She had no idea whether she had given Anthony what he needed. If it turned out that he had changed his mind or seemingly forgotten about a previous request, Rita felt that she had completely wasted the favor she had called in. Yet she was still on the hook for the trade she had struck with her colleague to get some help in fulfilling Anthony's request. Rita worried that people would start doubting that she knew what she was doing. "I was good at my job, but that was one of the most stressful periods of my professional life," she told us.

Even just knowing that someone can be unpredictable creates uncertainty as you anticipate disruptions to your plans. You worry about scenarios that may never happen, you invest extra time to prepare for all contingencies, and sometimes you have to abandon work you've already put time and effort into because shifts in demands have made the work unnecessary.

We are not suggesting that you simply challenge all requests from any authority figure who tends to be unpredictable. But you can make sure that you are communicating clearly to avoid chasing your tail. Far too often, busy managers are multitasking and overstretched and not fully aware of the collaborative demands of the work they are asking. They sometimes underestimate the impact of their requests. Quickly ensuring that you are on the same page with the prioritization or collaborative workload of a request can dramatically reduce downstream microstresses—but you have to catch this the moment someone asks.

In our research, we learned one quick hack to make sure you are aligned on requests. To help gauge the importance of the demand in real time, ask your manager to rate the new request on a ten-point scale. For example:

> **1** *means "I know this might be a wild idea, but it's something I would love for you to keep in the back of your mind."*

5 *means "This is something that we need to explore at some point."*

10 *means "This is a priority. I'd like you to work on this now, and I understand it will take priority over other work."*

You can then push back on the manager's 5 or 10 with your own rating of how difficult the idea would be to execute. In this way, your manager understands the trade-offs that need to be made to get that task done. This rating approach should help you have a quick, clarifying conversation to ensure that you and your manager are on the same page with your priorities and the best use of your time.

Keep track of all the requests (and the ratings). A visual rendering of the priorities can help a boss understand the full spectrum of requests made and make decisions more strategically. Without a visual representation, the tasks all seem small in isolation. When they are depicted visually with all the other ongoing demands, the impact can become far clearer.

Strategies to Push Back on an Unpredictable Authority Figure

Even well-intended leaders can unintentionally trigger microstress chaos when they don't stop to think about the consequences of what they're asking. In fact, you can make matters worse for yourself—and your manager—by always defaulting to "yes."

Understand How They Think

You don't have to wait for your leader to realize that the request was unreasonable. Get ahead of that by investing time in learning about your leader and what's important to their success. If you can better understand their needs and pain points, you may anticipate how things could shift.

Spend time learning about the broader context that drives work for your team and how your leader thinks about you and your team. With a better understanding of your boss's decision-making approaches, blind spots, and priorities that are driving their behavior, you may find the leader's decisions easier to predict. This understanding may also help you create counternarratives so that the leader who tends to easily accept direction from above is ready to defend you and your team instead.

Rebalance When Asked

Develop a habit of clarifying the time and resources that will be required to do something well. This assessment establishes an important baseline against which a new demand can be compared. Then, when requests change, you'll be in a better position to have a thoughtful conversation about how much time it will take to complete a new demand and what priorities may need to shift to accommodate it.

Engaging stakeholders in this kind of rebalancing may lead them to reduce what's being asked or take other work off your plate. Over time, it can also train them to be more aware of the impact of their requests and reduce the number of times they change directions.

Manage Your Emotions

Control your own emotions when responding to unpredictable shifts. Don't focus on being right, don't overreact, and don't let yourself get angry.

Instead of seeing the leader as the source of your problems, consider that they themselves might be stuck in an overwhelming pattern of demands. If you value the relationship, try to find positive ways of addressing what may well seem unreasonable.

Inefficient Communication Practices

We all complain about the volume and frequency of email (or instant messaging or any of the myriad other collaborative technologies) in our professional and personal lives. But in reality, it is not so much the specific technology platform (such as email or text) that kills us but the culture and norms around when and how we use it.

In fact, inefficient communication practices, which may be the most common of all the microstresses we have identified in our research, are draining our personal capacity because this microstress comes at us in increments of minutes or even seconds—but stretches on for hours or days. And this has only gotten worse through the Covid-19 pandemic as our days are typically packed with short, but more-intense meetings that are filled with microstresses. Studies have shown that the simple act of looking down at a text can consume sixty-four seconds of our attention as we try to reengage with a meeting or a problem we are trying to solve. If the disruption we experience is so great that we lose our train of thought, then the time to come fully back up to speed can be as much as twenty minutes! Do a quick estimate for yourself—how many small disruptions did you have yesterday? And how many big ones, as you tried to be responsive to others—like Rita's colleagues who dropped everything to respond to her request for help with the marketing manager's request? How much time did that add up to? This is how seemingly tiny microstresses rip through our days. Without consciously addressing communication norms with the people in your life, you are dooming yourself (and your colleagues) to late nights, early mornings, and an endless battering of unnecessary microstress!

Communication microstress comes from the feeling that you must respond quickly to texts, instant messages, and emails. Even tools that are intended to make your life easier, like videoconferencing, end up erasing your personal boundaries and making life harder by reducing your ability to multitask and chime in only when needed. In the end, you face considerable anxiety as you feel the need to be fully attentive to the myriad digital conversations across an amazing average of nine platforms that people need to monitor each day. Many of the people we interviewed told us that on a typical day, they don't even start their own work until 5 p.m. or later, after a day full of meetings, responding to emails, and so on. And starting your own work so late typically means putting in a second shift after your kids are in bed or after you've spent even a small amount of time catching up with your partner. Many of our high achievers defaulted to this method of working, convincing themselves that they were choosing to work this way. "I am willing to do a late-night shift because it allows me to have dinner with my family." Or "I'm a morning person. I just get up at 4:30 to get things done before my day kicks in." But that shouldn't be the only way to balance work and life.

People are always surprised by the degree to which small changes yield big differences. For example, one interviewee shared with us a simple process that dramatically changed her team's flood of inefficient communication. She called her team together for a brief meeting to present a PowerPoint slide with three columns. In the first column, she made a list of how the team currently collaborated. She included email, Slack, their internal team collaborative space, and so on.

For the second column, she asked the team for practices they wanted to follow. In the column across from the email entry, she wrote three bullet points: "State request and timeline in subject line," "Use bullet points where possible; no lengthy paragraphs," and "Move off email when we sense a disagreement; go to phone or video."

For the third column, she asked them to consider what current practices they wanted to discontinue as a team. She started them off with the email entry, too: "No email after 10 p.m., to avoid creating the expectation of an immediate response; send on timed delay if necessary," "Stop defaulting to copying everyone," and so on. The team immediately responded to her chart, adding to the first column the other ways they collaborated, such as video calls, phone, and meetings, and then suggesting other things to do and to stop doing (table 2-1). The review took less than an hour, but everyone was energized by the fact that they could exercise a bit of control for a change, laughing at some of the behavior they had fallen into, such as the constant "reply all" habit, which obliges people to endlessly chime in with "Sounds good" or "Thanks."

TABLE 2-1

Team review of collaboration methods: How to address our communication overload

How we collaborate	Practices we want to follow	Practices to discontinue
Email	• State request and timeline in subject line. • Use bullets where possible; no lengthy paragraphs. • Move off email when we sense a disagreement; go to phone or video.	• Stop defaulting to copying everyone. • Stop writing lengthy emails to clarify your own thinking. • Don't hide what you are asking for in the eighth paragraph. • No email after 10 p.m., to avoid creating the expectation of an immediate response; send on timed delay if necessary.
Meetings		
Instant messaging		
Team collaborative spaces		
Videoconferences		

"I think we managed to buy people back some real time," she told us. In fact, we helped her calculate that this simple act freed up at least 8 percent of her time—four or five hours in some weeks. But more importantly, it similarly freed up time for everyone on her team. "I thought it was just me who was always scrambling," she told us. "But someone who I thought of as a superconfident high performer privately told me that she was losing an hour or two a day and working late into the night trying to cc all or be responsive. This simple activity gave me a new lease on life."

Microstress 4: Inefficient Communication Practices

Most of us fall into the existing norms of our teams and our organizations without pausing to consider whether there's a more efficient way to communicate. But there are strategies to help you course correct.

Prune Collaborative Obligations: Be Proactive in Shaping Your Own Collaborative Work

Look at the past four months in your calendar for routine informational requests, decisions, and interactions that have become part of your role but that you could shift to less connected people to take demands off yourself and pull these people into the network. Look ahead two months for recurring meetings that you could shrink in time, spread further apart, or possibly cancel. Don't just look for the big items that are causing overload. Find the small ones that will cumulatively return a lot of time if you designate alternative go-to people or sculpt roles to remove yourself from the interactions.

Reduce Outbound Communications: Pay Attention to Your Own Communication Patterns

If your organization uses collaboration technologies that produce diagnostics, review yours to make sure that you aren't drowning your colleagues in emails, texts, and meetings. Alternatively, check in with peers who are doing similar work to get a sense of their communication cadence and email norms.

If you're sending out long emails far more frequently than others are, you may well be driving more demand back to you through your detailed requests or ambiguous directions. Reining in the pace and volume of communications can ease others' stress and your own, too.

Check Your Tendency to Jump In

Beware of any tendency to jump in when you shouldn't. We often get ourselves in trouble by engaging when we don't need to, because we get a sense of satisfaction from accomplishment. We like being recognized as the expert, or we get a sense of fulfillment from helping others. We might also jump in because we're driven by fear—fear of either being labeled a poor performer or missing out on opportunities. More-efficient collaborators are more aware of—and work to keep in check—any tendencies to create their own overload when they jump into unnecessary collaborations because of identity needs, fear, or excessive need for control.

A Surge in Responsibilities

The more things you are responsible for, the more that microstresses will emerge and cascade throughout discrete parts of your life in unexpected ways: having a child, moving, settling into a new job, taking on a significant volunteer project, and so on. Most of us recognize the toll these responsibilities take on our lives, and when these big transitions happen, our friends and family step up to support us. But surges in responsibilities come in smaller doses, too. Unlike a major life transition, with microstress surges, we just throw the extra responsibility onto our already-full plates without thinking about the cumulative load we are carrying.

Microstresses that increase our responsibilities at work are often exacerbated by the amount of time we need to collaborate with others. At a time when we are all expected to be agile, juggle multiple tasks, be part of numerous cross-functional teams, and respond to real-time demands from management and customers alike, surges in work often come from seemingly simple requests that don't factor in their complexity. Two projects can look identical in terms of the work required. But if one involves three functional areas across two time zones, two leaders who don't like each other, and the need for resources from a unit with different priorities, that's a different story. Such a project entails a massively greater workload than does a project with the same number of people in only one unit. Surges in responsibility create stress not only because of the actual work but also because of the collaborative footprint of the task.

Surges also occur in our personal lives and don't always come from immediate family responsibilities, such as being a parent or spouse. Microstress can also occur when we feel the burden of responsibility for extended family members, too. We might need to care for aging parents, and the stress can be exacerbated when relatives who aren't involved in your parents' day-to-day life freely weigh in with opinions but offer no help. Of course, surges never land on an empty plate. They cause some amount of stress purely because of the effort required to address them.

One interviewee described the burden of what she called *parent homework*, the assignments that your child brings home from school that are far beyond their capacity to complete independently. These tasks take planning and preparation and often force you to run out and buy last-minute supplies. (Have you ever tried to find poster board after eight o'clock at night?!) And the assignments always seem to creep up on you. For example, your child tells you Friday night that they have a big report due Monday, and your weekend is already crammed with plans. Adding even one extra project like that onto an already full to-do list can ripple stress throughout your whole family. Your child feels stress from your impatience or frustration with the project. Your spouse feels stress as you struggle to get the project done or ask them to step up to take care of it. You may cut corners at work because you're distracted and frustrated by this parent homework that suddenly appears. And the stress continues to generate ripples in your life.

The secondary effects of surges in responsibilities can be particularly damaging. Surges at work are bad enough, but perhaps even more painful is how they bleed into stress at home. When you're consumed with microstress from work, you aren't your best self at home. You may stay late at work or bow out of family obligations, disappointing everyone in the process. But even simply failing to give your family your full attention when you are home can profoundly affect your entire family's everyday happiness. Everyone feels it. And surges at home inevitably create stress at work—either because you have to work harder or because you need to manage disparate demands of work and home life. Working late at night and very early in the morning is bad for your brain; cortisol levels increase and you're exhausted. It's hard to be present in ways you should be at work and at home when you're constantly hanging on by a thread.

These stresses have become so commonplace that many people live their lives as one long string of microsurges in responsibilities, forcing them to react in ways that do the least damage. One interviewee told us that Sunday morning has become her favorite time to work. She used to enjoy both the spiritual and the social aspects of going to church, but now she doesn't have time for that. On Sunday mornings, she's likely to have had the first good night of sleep all week, and she can squeeze in a few hours of work before her family wakes up. She didn't even realize how much she'd allowed herself to put aside to make Sunday her best workday until we talked through the microstresses in her daily life.

Strategies for Pushing Back on Microstresses That Create Surges in Responsibilities

You can't always control what you're asked to do, but you can control how you respond. You don't have to default to yes. You can respond in ways that help you prevent a surge from taking over your life.

Push Back on Unreasonable Demands

Before people even ask, set expectations by clarifying the unique value that you add. This way, you ensure that they don't ask you to tackle something outside your areas of expertise. When possible, look to redirect work to someone who is in a better position to deliver what is requested. Be more confident in pushing back when others' demands are unreasonable. Finally, tap into your network for authoritative opinions

COACHING BREAK

Tracking the Surges in Your Life

To better understand how even small increases in responsibility are affecting your life, take note of the surges in demands on your time. They may seem tiny individually, but when you see them all on one page, the cumulative toll may be more obvious. Use a chart like the example in table 2-2 to prepare a helpful visual overview.

1. **Reflect on one or more surges in demand on your time.** Professionally, these surges might take the form of a new project that has a larger collaborative footprint than you realized, a promotion or shift in your role, or the need to cover for a colleague who has competing priorities or who left the organization. On the personal side, a friend or family member might be struggling with a setback, you might step into a leadership role in a nonwork group important to your identity, or you might be coping with shifting family responsibilities.

2. **Reflect on the full spectrum of relationships affected by this surge** and how these effects might create microstresses for you. Be diligent in seeing how one surge can affect relationships in—and cause stress from—the professional and personal sides of your life.

3. **Clarify how these affected relationships create microstress by draining your capacity.** Think about both the direct effect and the downstream stresses. For example, think about the effects on your personal relationships when you are juggling an unexpected responsibility at work. Not only will you likely add stress to your family's lives, but you may also be neglecting friends and other important relationships in your life when you're consumed with work.

4. **Identify actions that could help.** These actions might entail resculpting the work, securing additional resources for the task

to support you through a surge, or altering the interactions with people affected. We have some practical suggestions for this step in the next section.

TABLE 2-2

Sample personal microstresses chart

Step 1: Professional or personal surge	Rotation to new business unit as part of high-potential development path	Child suddenly struggling in school
Step 2: Relationships involved in surge	• New boss • New team • Spouse (absorbing more responsibilities because you're overloaded) • Children (because you are less present for them)	• Child • Spouse • Teacher • Child's siblings
Step 3: How these touch points create microstress	• Investing more time to understand role and build trust • Spending time to understand capabilities and aspirations on team • Diverting any time you would spend on yourself to make up for shortfall with family	• Time spent understanding struggle with child (and discussing with spouse) • Interactions with teacher to assess concerns and plot path forward • Time taken from child's siblings and interactions that created a positive family dynamic
Step 4: Ways to mitigate	• Tactically focus on behaviors that build competence and benevolent trust • Leverage former leader's expertise to understand team • Secure extra help at home (e.g., cleaner and grocery service) to create time during surge	• Engage in discussions as a full family to diagnose problems and create a supportive environment • Ask teacher to provide more timely feedback • Secure tutor for support and to separate this role from parenting role

or data and the backing of experts to legitimize your point of view when shifting unreasonable demands off your plate.

Be Held Accountable

Have people in your life who hold you accountable for not just saying yes to any request. Even well-meaning colleagues will take as much as you're willing to give; happier people tend to have others who help them make conscious decisions about what to give and what's not worth it.

The important people in your life, like your partner or other respected family members, can provide you with a kind of counterbalance when you are considering whether to jump into a major new commitment. They can help reinforce the importance of personal and family time to correct for the tendency to allow work to fill all available time.

Renegotiate Your Work Portfolio

Renegotiate other work demands the moment you're asked to handle a major surge of work. Instead of adding more to your workload without thinking, use that inflection point to get agreement on what can be taken off your plate or what resources you can receive to make the new request feasible.

. . .

Microstress from interactions that drain our capacity is pervasive in our professional and personal lives and takes an enormous toll on us. We end up in situations where we must work harder than anticipated on something—with the downstream consequences on other aspects of our lives—or we end up under-delivering. Either condition is stressful for us immediately, and each comes with secondary stresses, given the highly connected nature of our lives today. Targeted action can yield significant impact—as it can with the next category of microstresses: the interactions that drain our emotional reserves.

Chapter 3

Why Others Drain Your Energy

KEY INSIGHTS

- Professional interactions that create emotional burnout have grown exponentially in the past decade. But the **most emotionally draining microstresses can come at us from people we care deeply about**, including our closest colleagues, friends, and family.

- **Five common microstresses** deplete our emotional reserves but are not always obvious despite often reverberating in our lives for hours or days:

  - Managing and advocating for others
  - Confrontational conversations
  - Lack of trust
  - Secondhand stress
  - Political maneuvering

- **Our brains are highly sensitive to the emotions we pick up from others in our orbit.** We become stressed or anxious because other people are. When our mind is consumed with this form of microstress, we worry, we ruminate, and we absorb the microstress and, in turn, pass it on.

- **Push back on emotion-depleting microstress by altering the way you interact with people.** Increase your time with those who give you energy and bring you joy, and reduce your contact with people who dampen your spirit. In some cases, you may need to end your relationship with chronically negative influences.

- Research tells us that **negative interactions have as much as five times the impact of positive ones.** Removing even a few negative relationships can make a significant difference in your overall microstress level.

Emma was thrilled to have been recruited to a top leadership position at a national media company. The job required her to move to a different city, but the stress of making that move was more than offset by her enthusiasm for her new position and the company's mission. However, just days into the new post, it became clear that one of her new colleagues was not adjusting well to Emma's presence. Every morning, Emma's inbox was flooded with emails from this colleague, who often sent them well before 8 a.m. If she didn't respond fast enough, her colleague would pepper her with questions in meetings. He often repeated his requests on Slack in case she hadn't checked her email. Individually, none of the questions were unreasonable; they were small logistic questions. But her new colleague couldn't seem to settle into Emma's leadership. Her staff meetings would often shift from her predetermined priorities to a fire drill triggered by her anxious colleague. She endured this subtle badgering silently, seeking to calm him with reassuring answers. After all, she was trying to establish herself as a new leader. How would it look to her new team if she were rattled by what might seem to be basic demands of her new job?

Instead of sharing the excitement of her new dream job with her family, she found herself dominating the dinner table conversation with complaints about that one colleague. Her husband was quick to validate her feelings, but his response ended up reinforcing her sense of being a victim of this aggressive colleague and sent her into the office each day with built-up anxiety. She started to doubt her resolve and her own readiness for the new job. If she explained that this one colleague's constant questioning was driving her to the breaking point, it would sound ridiculous to outsiders, she thought. She was an experienced professional! Little by little, Emma began to question whether she was up to the job. She spent more time thinking about this one colleague than she thought about her entire team. In her first few months, she seriously contemplated quitting.

Emma's response might seem like an overreaction at first—she was going to quit a dream job because one colleague sent a lot of emails?—but not when we consider the toll of microstresses that drain our emotional reserves. This form of microstress is contagious. We pick up on anxiety, stress, happiness, and even fatigue simply by being around people who are feeling those things. And those negative cues, in turn, have a disproportionate impact on us.

There's a reason for that.

Over the past decade, science has shed light on how our brains are hardwired for emotional contagion—the way we respond to perceived emotions around us. Emotions spread via a wireless network of mirror neurons, which are tiny parts of the brain that allow us to empathize with others and understand what they're feeling. That's why when you see someone yawn, you feel like yawning, too. Mirror neurons activate in our own minds just from seeing someone else yawn.[1] Your brain picks up the fatigue response of someone sitting on the other side of the room. The same thing happens with smiles or laughter—our mirror neurons are triggered when we see someone else do that. But we can also pick up negativity, stress, and uncertainty like secondhand smoke. If someone in your visual field is anxious and highly expressive—either verbally or nonverbally—there's a high likelihood you'll experience those emotions as well, negatively impacting your brain's performance, according to researchers Howard Friedman and Ronald Riggio from the University of California, Riverside.[2]

Microstresses That Deplete Your Emotional Reserves

Like Emma, the leaders in our research expressed significant anxiety driven by confrontational conversations, politics, and concerns of falling short and letting their team down. Who hasn't allowed a passing comment or swipe from a colleague to rattle around in your mind for too long as you kick yourself for not saying the right thing in the moment?

None of the sources of microstress are the result of all-out political battles or toxicity from people trying to cause you pain. They're subtle, triggered by people in your everyday life, which is what makes them so tricky to spot and manage. In this chapter, we'll help you identify five microstresses that deplete your emotional reserves. We'll diagnose where they typically come from and offer practical steps you can take to push back or reshape your interactions to minimize the emotional toll.

Microstress 6: Managing and Advocating for Others

Getting promoted to a management position should be a happy event. But managing others and feeling responsibility for their success and well-being creates a unique drain on our emotional reserves as we manage performance issues, give critical feedback, or resolve group conflicts. No manager relishes giving a poor performance review. Even when done well, the task takes a toll before, during, and after the review itself. We worry about how the feedback will be received, whether we're being fair, the personal impact on the underperformer, and what it will mean to the future of the relationship. Just navigating the day-to-day challenges of feeling responsible for someone else's professional success can present us with an abundance of microstress.

Anxiety is driven by concerns of letting people down in both our personal and professional lives, especially when organizational circumstances out of our control play a role. One manager complained to us, "I had a hard time getting exceptional raises for people on my team who had had a great year, because that was how our company was. I always had a horrible feeling in the pit of my stomach when I went through the required talking points about why a 3 percent raise was a sign they were doing well."

There are also secondary microstresses that arise from managing, caring about, and advocating for others. These secondary microstresses might take several forms:

- **Falling short on coaching and development:** We know we *should* take the time to mentor and support our team, but we just can't get to it. As one interviewee put it, "It will take me an hour to do something that one of my junior team members will struggle to get done in three hours. It's just more efficient for me to do it myself." Skimping on subordinate coaching may be expedient in the short term, but it creates a host of other problems in the long term. By failing to take the time to help your team members develop, you are not only disappointing them but also making life harder for yourself. You are not developing the skills your team needs to succeed. You will, in effect, be making your job harder for yourself indefinitely. And as colleagues whom you care about have a more difficult time progressing in their careers, their stress and anxiety ricochet back on you. They give less effort and creativity to your projects and, in the extreme, might leave but only after we've carried the burden of some of their work (and the commensurate microstress) for far too long.

- **Draining political capital:** When you advocate for bonuses or promotions for your direct reports, you might create friction with other colleagues and your leaders. You might have to battle for limited promotion slots or bonus dollars. And once someone you have advocated for is promoted, their future success ends up being a reflection on your good judgment. If they underperform, it creates anxiety for you. Even just defending one of your team members when a senior colleague doesn't see their value the same way you do can cause you microstress.

- **Putting yourself last:** Think of how you might come home from work with a microstress rattling around in your brain, spurred by a brief text you got from a colleague during your slog of a commute. Feeling obliged to help your colleague can drive work into evenings and weekends, while your remaining emotional bandwidth will prioritize your family's needs ahead of your own. Putting others first is, of course, a noble endeavor, but it comes with the cost of scaling back on the people and activities that counterbalance your own microstress.

Consider what happened when a new manager who billed himself as a change agent started asking questions about Raoul's team's performance. In two decades with his financial services company, Raoul had helped his team survive multiple restructurings and layoffs over the years, and his teammates counted on him to keep them out of the fray of internal politics.

Raoul's new manager wanted to see innovation in his department's vendor relationships and seemed to be implying that Raoul's team wasn't up to the job. With every question from the manager, even casual ones, Raoul started to feel more protective of his team. He found himself spending inordinate amounts of time thinking about how to improve his manager's perception. He began to imagine problems that no one else on his team seemed to see, stepping in to help his team finish projects or overcompensating with his own time to make sure that the other departments they worked with felt that his team members were responsive.

As the nighttime and weekend work piled up, Raoul began to see that his instinctive attempts to protect his team were not taking a toll only on him but were also creating a situation that made his team vulnerable. "I was so worried about them that I was stepping in to solve what might not even be real problems and doing it too often," Raoul told us.

Strategies to Navigate Managing, Caring about, and Advocating for Others

Caring about the people you work with is part of what makes you a valued colleague. But that doesn't mean you have to let your protective feelings create layers of microstress for you—and inevitably your team, too. The trick is to help your colleagues grow without your needing to solve all their problems.

Create Shared Accountability

You can stop creating microstress if you stop trying to solve every problem on your own preemptively. Instead, find ways to inject guidance and accountability into everyday conversations. For example, expand traditional one-on-one interactions beyond mere work updates, and have good conversations about growth and development. Conversations like these let employees know you care and establish much more of a shared accountability for their development. Your team may surprise you by stepping up. You can also schedule your meetings for fifty minutes (instead of an hour) to create space for giving—and seeking—quick feedback. These real-time interactions provide the kind of nuanced, in-the-moment guidance and small course corrections that help people improve.

Coach for Independence

It can be easy to default to shielding your team from every possible setback both because you care about your people and because you want your team's performance to reflect your skills as a manager. But that stance can create ripples of microstress for you when you're unable to focus fully on your own work. Fight the urge to provide direction or help—even though this may seem more efficient or make you feel good in the moment. Instead, ask your team members to come back to you with their recommendation, and help connect them to resources they can use

COACHING BREAK

Avoiding the Triggers of Microstress

Are you unintentionally causing microstress for people you care about with well-intended protective behaviors? Professionally, we create microstress when we overprotect members of our team. They learn not to think for themselves, and they come back to us with increasingly small questions that fragment our days. And we create personal microstresses when we are overprotective with our children or overly empathetic with friends in ways that do not help them grow through difficult situations. As a result, our kids or friends rely on us even more in the future. As Raoul realized, this overprotective behavior almost always boomerangs. Recognizing how he was triggering microstress for others, he modified his behavior by answering the questions presented in tables 3-1 and 3-2. The overarching question is, who are you causing microstress for?

Tables 3-1 and 3-2 show how one high performer examined the microstress she was unintentionally causing others. This exercise can help you reflect on the interactions and behaviors where you may be overstepping—causing microstress and preventing the people in your life from taking advantage of opportunities to develop.

TABLE 3-1

Who are you causing microstress for at work?

WHAT YOU ARE DOING	CHANGE YOU CAN MAKE
Group affected: My team	
Second-guessing your team: I have undermined the confidence of my direct reports by anticipating problems or second-guessing their decisions without ever making clear to them why I'm concerned.	Select low-profile delegation opportunities and step back. Celebrate the creativity that emerges, and don't comment on how I would have done it differently.
Person affected: My boss	
Offering help beyond my capabilities: With good intentions, I'm taking on obligations beyond what I and my team are capable of delivering. Ironically this ends up letting my boss down. This habit also creates secondary stress in my team, as they are overwhelmed and unable to complete work at a level of quality they feel good about. It also creates secondary stress at home through late nights and missed family obligations.	Help my boss understand the full collaborative and work demands of her assignments. Use small moments of the request to determine the true priorities at the time of all work commitments to keep from overloading myself and my team and to help my boss make more-informed assignments in the future.
Group affected: My peers	
Volunteering to help too many people: I focused on building my network of peers in my new job by understanding their core priorities and pain points and offering to help. This strategy was effective in helping me fully join the team and integrate myself into the company, but now I'm overloaded and overwhelmed. As a result, I'm actually not only not helpful to my peers, I am actively letting them down by making promises I can't keep to help with work that isn't actually aligned with my own career growth. I don't see the "win" for anyone here. I need to be less quick to volunteer help and resources that don't align with my goals and desired career path.	Take time to clarify three to five capabilities I want to use in my work and the values I want to experience in my career. Be more cautious of jumping in to help in situations that do not advance these aspirations. Be more proactive in scheduling meetings and initiating work that satisfies these desires.

(continued)

TABLE 3-2

Who are you causing microstress for at home?

WHAT YOU ARE DOING	CHANGE YOU CAN MAKE
Group/person affected: Significant other	
Fueling wounded feelings: I overemphasize empathy in interactions with my significant other but don't complement these interactions with a discussion of a path forward. That feels good in the moment, because I am supporting them. But it is driving more and more interactions back to me because my partner is not seeing or owning the part of the problem they are creating and is falling further into victim mode.	We will agree to a time in our discussions—in either one interaction or a couple of them—where we move from empathy to problem-solving. We will create a code word to hold each other accountable for creating truly supportive interactions and not ones that simply enable the persistence of microstress.
Group/person affected: Close friend	
Being on call 24-7 for friends: I have fallen into a pattern of being available to a close friend immediately at any time of the day or night. She was going through a difficult divorce, and I helped her move through this phase of life. But as things have stabilized, she has become too reliant on my help. Her overdependence not only creates more stressful interactions between her and me but also causes disappointment in my family and leaves me neglecting my own life priorities.	I will ask more questions about what she thinks she needs to do rather than jump in too quickly to help. In this way, I will work to help her diagnose and solve her own problems rather than relying on me to do so.
Group/person affected: Child	
Solving every problem: I have gotten too directive on what my second child should be doing with his natural talents. I view this tendency as protecting him for the future as he takes care of academics and extracurricular activities that will get him into the best school. But my narrow lens on what is his best path to success (the best college) is creating stress in our relationship and myriad microstresses from the activities I have to help him coordinate.	I will begin to push him to be more accountable for his own course in life. To this end, I will ask more questions so that he is directing what he thinks is important and to make him accountable for those spheres. Through these efforts, he will learn to be self-directed and not overly reliant on me.

to solve the problem. If there's a better person to help them build their capability and decrease their reliance on you, connect them. Or arrange team-based coaching relationships that help distribute these interactions across the team—enabling more-experienced employees to provide mentoring. Team members may initially resist these efforts if they have become too used to having you solve their problems, but the benefits for their career and the capability you're building in the team will outweigh any short-term inefficiencies.

Be Transparent about Your Limits

Trying to make everybody happy all the time will trigger waves of microstress for you: fear of letting people down, constant rumination over other people's performance problems, anxiety about looking weak as a manager. If you're transparent and honest and develop genuine relationships, you're less likely to experience microstress. Find ways to put your role and responsibilities in context so that you don't overburden yourself. Communicate to the people involved how much time you have for each responsibility, and engage them in identifying what you should focus on to make the best use of that time. In the end, there's only so much you can do for your teams; each day, you must pick a point to shut off and say, "I've done what I can today." Not only will allowing yourself to "turn off" work at the end of the day help reduce the likelihood that you'll bring all your microstresses home to your family at night, but doing so will also send a powerful signal to your colleagues that they, too, are allowed to have limits. One manager routinely told his team when he had to wait home for a repairman the next day or deal with a battery of medical appointments for his child specifically so he would send the message that it's OK to focus on personal priorities sometimes, too.

Microstress 7: Confrontational Conversations

Being on the receiving end of someone's anger or losing your cool with a colleague or loved one never feels good. But we sometimes disregard the smaller, subtler confrontational conversations that we have every day. We're not talking about angry customers or peer bullies. We're talking about microstress triggered by everyday interactions with colleagues and peers: competing goals, misaligned cultural values, personality differences. You might find yourself exhausted after what should be routine interactions with colleagues, simply because you approach problem-solving differently. Or you might feel so protective of your team that you find yourself interpreting passing comments about them from other team leaders as criticism that might not be intended. You are always more guarded than you want to be.

Yuhan shared with us a litany of small moments of confrontation that she'd had to cope with in her current position as a finance manager in a global logistics organization. "They're just part of my job, but those kinds of interactions ruin my day," she told us. "I'll replay them in terms of how I could have been more effective, and I'll take that home with me and then continue to play it out—even for the whole weekend, when I really should be focusing on my family." She often had to respond to colleagues who groused to her about having their budgets reduced or expenses questioned, even when the decisions were not hers. "None of these conversations were extraordinary in a growing company like mine," she said. "But over the course of a week or a month, cumulatively they started to wear me down."

There are myriad ways in which people who are trying to get their work done can find themselves in subtle forms of confrontation with others trying to do the same. Perhaps you are being challenged by a colleague who has different performance incentives or are navigating work-style differences with people around you. Individually, each of these microstress moments might feel like a routine work exchange to an outsider. But they can be the source of angst or anger that lingers for a long while. You find yourself worrying before you even have the confrontation—gaming your possible responses and approaches to ensure that you aren't steamrollered by the other person. Or you might not like how you handled the confrontation in the moment, losing your cool, responding with inappropriate petulant behavior, or simply failing to communicate your point of view clearly. And after a confrontational conversation, most of us find ourselves mentally replaying what happened, amplifying the wrong we felt or kicking ourselves for not saying the right thing in the moment. Even subtle confrontations can stir up emotions for the rest of the day.

They also trigger a series of secondary microstresses, too, including:

- **Emotional exhaustion:** Doing extra work to prepare for the conversation and mentally managing the anticipation of the interaction, even if it's a minor quibble, is exhausting. Who hasn't woken up in the middle of the night, replaying a conversation that they wished they had handled better and tensing up in the process? The effects may linger for days. You can't stop ruminating about the conversation, and when you pass on the secondhand stress to colleagues around you, their energy and focus may be affected as well.

- **Open-ended tension:** Even minor confrontations create additional tensions that come from the need to follow up to make sure that progress is being made on what was discussed or that the problem has indeed been resolved. Adding formality and lack of trust into a working relationship can keep tensions simmering long beyond the original source of conflict. You may find that colleagues try to avoid working with you when they can; the strain can affect your reputation and the potential for growth opportunities at work.

- **Disruption of personal life:** Many of us tend to prep for our confrontations and then replay them with our loved ones to try to release the emotions involved. But this habit can be a frustrating experience for our partners, who feel powerless to help in complex situations beyond their control. Their emotional fallout from our own poor mood can further magnify the original stress we felt.

Taking the Microstress Out of Confrontational Conversations

Try to get ahead of a likely confrontational conversation by identifying two or three things you can do to minimize microstress at each stage—before, during, and after. Here are some specific suggestions.

Before the Confrontation

One of the most effective techniques to prevent microstress-level conflicts from triggering a cascade of other microstresses is to *create alignment in advance.* Sharing a common vision of what you are trying to achieve limits the risk of misalignments in the first place. You can get a range of people in your professional life on board with your vision:

- **Leaders:** Invest in understanding your leaders' priorities and pain points so that you are better able to help them succeed and can decrease the likelihood of confrontational conversations around performance expectations.

- **Peers:** With your peers, be quick to establish mutually beneficial priorities and clarity on joint commitments to remove two of the most common drivers of confrontational conversations—times when people do not benefit in the way they should or when colleagues are not coming through.

- **Team members:** Keep open channels of communication with your team members, and encourage them to share concerns and problems early on, before these issues become significant points of contention.

- **Other influencers:** Actively seek out and engage informal opinion leaders who might be negative influencers—that is, those who may be pulling in different directions or who care about different aspects of the work. Invest time in meeting with them to understand their positions, find common ground, balance each of your priorities, and work together to cocreate solutions that incorporate both your ideas and theirs so that conflicts won't arise in the first place.

Before an anticipated confrontation, also *focus on what you can control.* If you expect a difficult conversation, try to take control of the timing. Don't avoid the conversation, but try to initiate it when you're calm and ready for the discussion rather than having an exchange sprung on you at an inopportune moment.

During a Confrontation

When you are in a confrontational discussion, *focus on, and establish, the facts.* Review the basics of what is creating the conflict. Often, the context of the conflict has nothing to do with either you or your colleague personally. Amy Gallo, author of the *HBR Guide to Managing Conflict*, suggests using a few simple phrases to keep your conversation focused on the facts of the conflict, rather than getting personal:

- "Here's what I'm thinking."

- "My perspective is based on the following assumptions . . ."

- "I came to this conclusion because . . ."

- "I'd love to hear your reaction to what I just said."

- "Do you see any flaws in my reasoning?"

- "Do you see the situation differently?"

Try to get to a common understanding of the facts with the other person during your conversation, rather than focusing on trying to be right.

(continued)

After a Confrontation

After any contentious discussion, you must work hard to *avoid replaying the interaction* in your own mind or rehashing it with others—all you will do is magnify points you already worry over. Check back in with the other person with an offer of resources or other help or to share the progress on your commitment. This practice helps ensure that the discussion stays focused on the work. And finally, try to celebrate the actions that both of you are taking by involving others so that positive behavior is encouraged.

Build a back-channel source of information from your network. This source can come from others who know the person with whom you're having conflict. If you're having genuine problems with that person, it's likely that others are as well. These people's advice can be valuable if they understand the person and situation well. They may have useful guidance on how to resolve the issue. Or they may help you see that you aren't at fault. Just knowing that you aren't the source of the problem can reduce the emotional impact of the conflict and help you respond more rationally.

Microstress 8: Lack of Trust

When others trust us, they are more willing to take risks on our behalf. They will engage in honest debate with us, and they are likely to spread the good word about who we are and what we have accomplished. When we've worked side by side with people for months or years, we build trust. We know our colleagues well enough to know when we can count on each other and for what.

Lack of trust, conversely, can affect both our colleagues' performance and our own. In these situations, it is not the conventional form of stress we have all felt when we distrust someone or perceive them to have poor intent. Rather, this is a form of microstress created by the absence of trust. Unfortunately, trust does not come easily in many working relationships, because of the dynamics of virtually all modern workplaces, where working groups form and re-form and people move rapidly out of teams and often have competing priorities. Microstress can be triggered simply because we don't know our colleagues well enough to know their capabilities or because we are unsure about whether they have our best interests in mind. Or we just don't know if we can count on a colleague to deliver on their commitments. And of course, with the pandemic-induced rise of remote work, where our interactions are less rich and more prone to misinterpretation, we've further limited the ability to build trust with our colleagues through working together.

Consider how lack of trust affected Bill, a senior analyst in a consulting firm. As his company began to focus on more agile ways of working, where teams were assembled, disassembled, and reformed quickly, Bill had gotten used to working with an ever-shifting cast of colleagues. He rarely had time to learn his team's and colleagues' capabilities before he was working with a new group. And though he had been with the company for years, many of his newer colleagues lacked a good understanding of what he was capable of. With each shift, he felt as if he were starting from scratch, both in learning what he could rely on from his teammates and in ensuring that they knew his own strengths and limitations. Because of this uncertainty, he had to spend more time checking in, making sure the work was aligned with the group's objectives, and worrying about the quality of the output that would come his way. These three extra concerns arose not because of anything nefarious but because the rapid shifting of teammates took away Bill's trust in others' abilities. He wasted inordinate amounts of time second-guessing and double-checking the work of his colleagues so that his own work would not somehow be affected as a result. Microstress in layers ensued.

An absence of trust can also produce several secondary microstresses:

- **It can drive work back to us.** What we're talking about here is subtle—not the result of a fundamental level of mistrust. When we don't know our colleagues well enough to understand how they work, their strengths and weaknesses, and how we can work best together, we tend to do things ourselves—after all, we know what we're capable of. Though this approach might feel efficient in the short term, it unfortunately increases our stress as we're robbing Peter to pay Paul—our main work is still there, needing to get done. This lack of appropriate delegation can also sap our colleagues' energy and engagement. They are taught to be passive about doing work themselves and active about asking us to resolve small questions for them. And the same can be true when others treat us this way. Why bother killing ourselves to make something great when a colleague is going to go over it with a fine-tooth comb anyway?

- **It can make us neglect important priorities.** What we don't trust gets our focus at the expense of all else. Bill, for example, continually ignored his manager's request to think more strategically, because he was constantly consumed with daily assignments and checking on team members he didn't sufficiently trust. As a consequence, when the manager turned to someone else in the department to help plan how the department would juggle the workload during a particularly busy period, Bill himself was loaded up with even more work.

- **It can make us sabotage our own advancement.** If others begin to see us as unhelpful or resistant because of our trust issues, we may not be given chances to grow or advance in our organizations. Because Bill spent so much time double-checking and second-guessing other colleagues, both his manager and his colleagues began to wonder if he was a dinosaur, stuck in doing things the old ways. Despite his considerable experience, Bill watched several colleagues move into management roles although he had never been given the chance to do so himself.

Strategies to Build Trust

You can rapidly build trust with your colleagues in ways that don't rely on years of side-by-side work or doing trust falls at retreats. You just have to see trust in a new light. Here are the four key areas in which you can actively work to build trust so that your daily interactions are not laden with microstresses triggered by lack of trust.

Situate Your Capabilities in the Context of Other People's Needs

Rather than proclaiming your expertise to all who will listen, figure out where your skills and capabilities fit into your colleagues' needs. Focus on those areas. Set up exploratory meetings, ask a lot of questions, and find ways that your capabilities can be useful in helping others to meet their goals. Create mutual wins, and credit others for shared accomplishments. For example, when a job change meant that Azzam, an experienced product development manager, had to build trust from scratch with a new team, he focused on finding opportunities to show where he could add value. He set up "town meetings" with his team, where they could ask any question. Initially his team members were polite, but over time they asked more-challenging questions. As he made clear how his previous experience could help support the work they were doing now, they began to understand what they could count on Azzam to provide.

Establish Competence-Based Trust

People develop competence-based trust in you when they believe that you know what you are talking about and have the skills to get the job done. This kind of trust arises, in part, when you display your capabilities and perform well in projects and assignments. Don't simply say "I can do that" and expect people to believe you. Show evidence of where you have done it before or a prototype of what is possible. Concrete evidence quickly moves people from questioning whether they can trust in your abilities to looking at your already-accomplished work and reflecting on how it can be applied to their problem. You can also help people learn to trust you by being candid about the boundaries of your expertise—that is, what you really are good at and what you may not be proficient doing. By clarifying your unique value and not weighing in on things outside your expertise, you avoid being pulled into work for which you are not the best person. Your willingness—in appropriate situations—to acknowledge the gaps in your own knowledge or expertise increases other people's trust in what you say you do know. And it encourages them to be vulnerable and authentic as well. Trust is built on those kinds of authentic connections.

Azzam established competence-based trust by drawing parallels between his current group's work and the work he had led at his previous organization. He found occasions to offer up solutions or experiences he'd had, to solve something the team was struggling with. And he further created trust by acknowledging the domains in which he was not an expert.

Demonstrate Reliability

Deliver on your promises, and be realistic when setting expectations, even when it means pushing back or telling a senior leader something they don't necessarily want to hear. In the town meeting and outside of it, Azzam established a policy of candor with his team. He kept teammates posted about any changes that might affect them, gave them clear answers about his and other leaders' expectations, and made a point of keeping his word once he gave it. Over a few months, he went to bat for his team several times, demonstrating that he would indeed keep his word.

Build Benevolence-Based Trust

This sort of trust is based on people's belief that you have a genuine concern for the well-being of others. When working with colleagues or customers, get to know the whole person—not just the side of someone who delivers on tasks—by periodically stepping out of your role and connecting on nonwork subjects, such as hobbies, interests, or aspirations. Show an interest in people, and connect with them off-task—even when your commonality has yet to be discovered. Benevolence-based trust is triggered when people feel a connection and find things in common outside the purely functional demands of their day-to-day work. As he was learning about his new team, Azzam spent time with them informally, too. He organized a brown-bag lunch every two weeks, finding a conference room with a view and asking any of his colleagues who were available to join him. They talked about sports, hobbies, their families, and so on, establishing personal connections beyond the work.

Building trust requires you to allow yourself to be authentic with the people around you. You don't have to go all in to build a deep trust with colleagues. But you can find small ways to make things better. When others trust you, they are more willing to take risks on your behalf. They will engage in honest debate with you, confident that you share a commitment to advancing a common good, and they are likely to spread the good word about who you are and what you have accomplished. Among the people we interviewed, their personal growth and their ability to apply their skills and interests in ways that suited their values and aspirations relied heavily on the base of trust they had cultivated with others. In fact, people were sometimes offered new opportunities simply on the basis of the leader feeling *I need someone I can trust.*

As we have shown, trust can be built in a progression of stages. You don't need to rely on years of working side by side to create the kind of trust that longtime colleagues have in one another. You can build trust in stages that focus on the skills and capabilities you bring to the work.

Microstress 9: Secondhand Stress

Most of us have had to work with leaders, colleagues, or even junior teammates who wear their stress on their sleeve—these people just radiate stress. Somehow, our own anxiety is escalated by the constant spray of stress and worry that these colleagues throw off. Even their body language and tone of voice can get to us. We pick up on their microstress and make it our own.

Secondhand microstress affects us directly in many ways. We might get nervous about completing team deliverables when peers' stress makes us wonder whether they'll pull through in time. Or we may become anxious that a direct report is so stressed that they may drop the ball and make us look bad. Secondhand microstress spreads when people voice fear of missing deadlines, claim that the proposed next steps will never work, or show their stress by recounting their workload to others. But it also spreads through physical cues like voice inflection and other ways, like the pace and time of electronic communications. Merely observing someone who is stressed—especially a coworker or a family member— can have an immediate effect on our own nervous systems. One group of researchers found that 26 percent of people showed elevated levels of cortisol *just by observing someone who was stressed.*[3] Worse yet, technology lets us broadcast our aggressive voice or constant questions to many people all at once.

Secondhand microstress can also create several less obvious but equally challenging downstream stresses:

- **Secondhand microstress can burn out our creative spark.** Increased microstress decreases creative thinking and new ideas—an effect that has been shown many times in psychology research. Diminished creativity in turn may make you less appealing to a team working on creative, engaging projects. Moreover, teams that experience high levels of secondhand stress are more distracted and less effective interpersonally and often experience a drop in productivity.

- **It threatens to amplify our anxiety.** Secondhand microstress ramps up as it is passed from one person to another and can rebound to us over time. Without an identifiable source of anxiety, we are exposed to others' anxious behaviors; we internalize their stress and pass it on to others. It's like an emotionally charged game of telephone, where each person passes on stress to the next person, in a cycle that further ramps up in the messaging. Remote work has only exacerbated this problem. Because most virtual interactions are scheduled, we miss the many small chances to notice someone's stress signals early on, when it's possible to deal with the stress before it spreads.

- **Secondhand stress can kill our motivation.** When we work in environments where anxiety propagates through our interactions with highly stressed individuals or even when we simply observe others who are anxious, we can start wondering if it's worth all the stress. We take shortcuts, stop caring about the quality of our own work, give less than our best because we are absorbing so much secondhand microstress, and decide that the work is not worth the commitment.

For many of us, the Covid-19 pandemic offered daily secondhand microstress. Take Jasmine, a manager in a well-known consulting firm. The secondhand stress from her team almost derailed her. When the pandemic hit, all sixty people in her group started working from home. As the health crisis dragged on, Jasmine could see the cracks forming for people on her team, especially for dual-income employees who now had to also take care of children 24-7 because daycare options were limited and all the schools had turned to remote learning.

At the peak of the pandemic, Jasmine estimated that she spent half of her time talking to her people, trying to help them as they navigated the complexities of delivering quality work from home while also taking care of children. Seeing how much they were struggling to manage work and family—and feeling guilty that her children were teenagers and didn't need the same level of attention—left her losing sleep and having trouble staying focused and motivated. Her employees' anxiety became her anxiety. And her anxiety, however she tried to hide it, was fueling theirs even more. "I felt caught in an endless cycle of small stresses," she told us. "And that spilled out into my home life, too. I couldn't even stay focused on my yoga, which had been an important escape for me. My mind just kept wandering back to my team and what I was or wasn't doing to help them."

Too often people suffer the effects of exposure to secondhand microstress and assume there's little they can do about it. But making some small changes in how you—and others—engage can significantly reduce exposure to secondhand stress and improve everyone's quality of work (and home) life.

Strategies to Push Back on Stress Contagion

It's all too easy to get sucked up into someone else's microstress. But if you're aware that it's happening, you can find ways to keep that secondary microstress from seeping into your days that are already filled with primary microstress.

Don't Propagate the Stress Cycle

Check your own emotional reaction. Take a moment to calm and recenter yourself, if need be. Don't let others' stress elevate yours into an unproductive or defensive posture that further propagates the secondhand-stress cycle. Focus on your breathing, go for a walk, inject humor into a conversation, or use any other approach that dissipates the stress and helps you be positively present in the situation.

Engage with Empathy

Approach the situation with an empathic lens that doesn't blame others. Recognize that they are probably just displacing stress that comes from the pressures they feel from expectations and time constraints. Work with them to uncover nonobvious drivers of stress in their lives. Lead the conversation with curiosity to understand what's driving their stress.

The thing that is causing people stress often emanates from a different source. Understanding their intentions in the stressful situation can help you coach them on how they might execute on those intentions without externalizing their stress to people around them.

For example, stress might be spreading not because of a demanding client but because a person is not good at prioritizing. High performers often take too much on and sometimes can't deliver the quality they should.

Coach Others to Curb Contagion

To help people understand how their secondhand stress affects others, describe how it has affected you. Using *I* statements, describe your own emotional reactions to their secondhand stress and the specific impacts that it produces in your life. The challenge here is that people may get defensive if they see your comments as critical of them personally or if they can't see how their behaviors are creating stress for others in the first place. But if they understand the impact that their stress is having on colleagues, they tend to be more open to containing rather than externalizing their stress.

Microstress 10: Political Maneuvering with Your Boss, Peers, or System of Connections

Few of us are immune to the stresses of working in an environment where decisions seem political or blatantly unfair. Competitive colleagues can consume our energy but not always in open-warfare ways. Political maneuvering can be extremely subtle but still powerful. Myriad small, implied, or subtle forms of political maneuvering reverberate in our lives.

You may sense an unspoken agenda and spend a tremendous amount of time worrying about and engaging with others to try to get a sense of the political lay of the land. Or you may notice that people find ways to subtly elbow their colleagues out of the pole position for C-suite attention. This political maneuvering can create microstress in several ways. For example, we experience anxiety whenever we sense that something is going on but we don't fully understand whose opinion matters or the underlying agendas that are driving different conversations. We certainly experience microstress when we are pressured to support goals or actions that we don't believe in or ones that put us in conflict with other groups. And simply realizing that, somehow, political maneuvering means we don't have as much control over our careers as we once thought can also create stress as we second-guess every situation and do more work than is necessary just to cover all bases.

Consider the scenario Connor found himself having to navigate. Connor and several of his colleagues had been cc'd on a back-and-forth debate between his manager and a manager in a different division of the company on a joint project. The two managers were publicly debating how to handle a difficult resource allocation question that involved

Connor's time. The other manager kept demurring—over email to the entire group—avoiding a direct answer. A couple of those cc'd on the email chain dared to wade in with comments, which only seemed to escalate the situation. Finally, one colleague suggested that the two managers take the disagreement offline.

It wasn't the first time Connor had seen the two managers battling over his time and work. Disagreements were usually subtle, sometimes passive-aggressive, but it was clear to everyone on that email chain that the two managers were annoyed with one another. When Connor's direct manager seemed to push the other manager for resolution, the other manager seemed to work even harder to avoid responding to his query.

Connor worried about the conflict privately with several of his peers, discussing in hushed tones what was going on. "This is so awkward for me," he said. He wondered if he had done anything to trigger the battle. He started overthinking every email he was about to send. Should he cc them both? Just his manager? "This debate was about my time," he told us, "but they clearly couldn't agree, and it escalated quickly. It was really uncomfortable."

Most of us have had experiences where we slowly come to grasp that something's going on that we don't fully understand. Being caught in political maneuvering, whether directly or indirectly, can generate second-order stress in various ways:

- **It can amplify our own stress.** When we share our sense of unfairness about political maneuvering with friends or significant others, their automatic instinct is to empathize with us. But because they often lack any context around the larger situation, their responses reinforce our own belief that a situation is unfair or that the system is stacked against us. Their well-meaning responses only serve to deepen our stress and anger. In our efforts to diffuse some of our stress caused by the maneuvering around us, we make things worse by adding fuel to our emotional fire.

- **We can get stuck in a burnout loop.** When politics denies us the resources we need to succeed—budget, sponsorship, vital

information, and so on—we find ourselves and our teams working harder than usual to make up for the shortfall. Overwork, of
course, will eventually catch up with us. Feeling as though we're
not being dealt a fair hand at work and then having to overcom-
pensate for that perceived unfairness leads to more stress and
burnout.

- **Political maneuvering can remove us from the inner circle.** Continually finding ourselves on the losing end of political schemes can
make us feel like an outsider in our own organization. We're not
talking about coming up short in a major political battle in which
there are winners and losers, such as getting a plum promotion
over an internal rival. We're referring to the more subtle forms of
political maneuvering, such as budget decisions and recognition
and support for our initiatives—interactions that ultimately affect
our own sense of where we fit in. We become increasingly uncertain about how to position our projects to gain others' support,
and we second-guess ourselves at every turn. Our stress levels
rise as we get caught in a negative reinforcing cycle that is hard to
break out of. It undercuts our ability to work effectively and alien-
ates us from our own organizations.

Connor didn't want to be caught up in the subtle power struggle between two leaders. So, he resolved to do things differently. The next
time he was selected to work on a cross-unit project, he started working
his network early and proactively to make sure his project would be a
success.

His first step was to figure out what the political issues around his new
project might be. To do this, he booked meetings with both functional
leaders and informal opinion leaders in the organization to gather their
input on the new project. He got a feel for potential red flags or subtle
agendas that he could navigate once he understood what was at play.

Through these conversations, Connor realized that some minor
changes to the scope of the project at the outset would help reassure
several key leaders and would thereby help secure their political support.

These changes would have very little impact on the overall goals but would help clear the path so that the project would not die a death of a thousand cuts.

"You would think that building these coalitions and working through others would increase my stress by turning the project into some kind of high-stakes political battle," Connor told us. "But instead, just the opposite happened. My contacts did things that they were comfortable with once they saw how our interests were aligned. And as a result, my life actually got simpler and less stressful."

Strategies to Avoid Being Caught in Political Maneuvering

However subtle a political skirmish can be, a person feeling caught in the crosshairs of an unspoken power struggle can endure waves of microstress. You start to worry about what you know, what you don't know, what you can control, and what you can't. But you don't have to let that happen.

Enroll Key Influencers

Get ahead of the politics by enrolling key influencers—those well-connected people who sway many others. Begin by meeting with each of the most obvious people who will influence the trajectory of your work. To discover other key influencers whom you may not know about, at the end of each meeting, ask who else would care about this topic and who might have slightly different priorities that could undermine progress. You will almost always be pointed in the direction of opinion leaders who can have a disproportionate impact on other people's acceptance of your plans and ideas.

Then, meet with those influencers to understand their core priorities or pain points, and find ways to help solve their problems. Offer them assistance in areas where you have competence, and maintain your relationship with them over time. A little time and proactivity like this up front can encourage these influencers to support your efforts rather than slowly derailing good ideas.

Work through Mutual Contacts

Influence political players indirectly through your mutual contacts. The key is to find out whom these people are influenced by—sometimes it's a chief of staff, someone they have worked with in the past, or a personal confidant. Then seek ways to deliver messages through these people. In one of our interviews, a manager described how she had worked through her previous leader, who had considerable sway with someone she was trying to influence and who could seed the right story and perspective with that person on her behalf. Her former leader presented the same information that she would have presented. But coming from a different person created buy-in that she would have struggled to get directly.

Separate Positions from Interests

Use your connections to understand the histories and hidden motivations of people who are engaged in political maneuvering. Beneath every clearly stated position—for instance, "That unit should report to the CFO!"—is an underlying interest. In this case, perhaps, the underlying conviction is a belief that inconsistent financial decisions are hurting the organization and need to be addressed. How do you discover these underlying interests? You use your mutual contacts—people who understand the situation more deeply and who can help you position your efforts appropriately.

. . .

The microstresses that deplete your emotional reserves can be even more challenging than those that drain your capacity. Some of the most miserable people in our research were those who—with good intentions—simply absorbed the blows of microstresses that left them running on empty rather than finding ways to navigate the stress. Over time, their lack of a proactive response had a chilling effect on the quality of their lives. They used up all their emotional bandwidth to fend off these microstresses.

But there is an even more taxing form of microstress. It's the kind that challenges your identity. We'll explore how this microstress plays out in the next chapter.

Chapter 4

Why You Don't Feel Like *You*

 **KEY INSIGHTS**

- **The demands of the roles we play—at work and at home—often put us in conflict with who we set out to be in our lives.** At work, these demands might come from expectations to pursue business objectives that conflict with our values or to operate in high-pressure or toxic situations that undermine our confidence. At home, we frequently have unrealistic expectations of who we are supposed to be as spouses, parents, friends, and siblings, and we beat ourselves up for seemingly not being good enough at anything.

- **People rarely slip away from the person they wanted to be with one decision that fundamentally changes who they are.** Rather, the change happens over time in many small choices—ones we often justify as necessary to provide for our family or to pursue a given career trajectory.

- Four common sources of microstress challenge your identity:

    ◦ Conflict with your personal values
    ◦ Undermined confidence

  ○   Draining or other negative interactions with family or friends
  ○   Disruptions to your network

- Finding ways to change your interactions with people who are pushing you away from the person you want to be can have a dramatic impact on your sense of purpose in life. You can try to reshape your role, change how you interact with colleagues or loved ones, or find small ways to express your values outside of your core job. Subtle changes can make a significant difference.

R achel had wrestled with misgivings from the start. When her boss suggested her for a promotion into management at her midsize bank, Rachel shared her concern that she lacked experience that the new role required. "Rachel, you're a star," her manager assured her. "You have been flagged as a high potential. I have the utmost confidence in you!" Her manager made clear that Rachel had the support of other senior leaders in the company. Putting her doubts aside, she accepted the job, which was a significant increase in responsibilities.

But once she was in the new position, she began to feel uncomfortable. Now she was having to say no to people and rapidly make decisions about project priorities and promotions. Her choices affected people she cared about profoundly. She knew, of course, that these decisions would be part of the job, but the speed at which she was expected to make them, and the tone she was supposed to convey in them, felt wrong to her. "I hate confrontation," she confessed to us. She had become adept at working through problems more diplomatically. "Over the years, I had become pretty effective at working with people without needing to resort to being confrontational," she explained. In the new job, she wanted to be fair and thoughtful. She would refrain from making snap decisions about anything, allowing her team to provide input into her decisions and occasionally changing her own opinion after she'd had some feedback.

A few months into the new job, however, her manager told her she wasn't being assertive enough. "Rachel, this is a fast-paced business," her boss told her. "You have to ask for what you want in no uncertain terms. I need you to rise to the challenge of being a manager!" Rachel was rattled. She believed she could accomplish her goals through building strong relationships with her team and not through mandates. "It was a slap in the face to me," she told us. "It was like, 'Yeah, even though you got this job on merit, you can't be the same you that you were before. That's not good enough.'" As Rachel saw it, it wasn't a matter of simply needing to grow into the demands of the new job. "He wanted a mini-me," she said. "Someone who was just as confrontational as he was."

At first, she blamed herself for not being managerial enough and began to follow his lead. She found herself sending less-than-diplomatic emails, stopping colleagues in the hallways to brusquely check in on their work without even asking how they were doing, or mimicking her manager's curt tone in meetings so as not to be seen as a pushover. Every day, she felt a bit more miserable. The people on her team she once considered friends had distanced themselves from her. She watched them gather for lunch without inviting her. She would arrive home from work, emotionally depleted and unable to engage with her family until she had decompressed with a drink. She began to miss book-group meetings with last-minute excuses that she had too much going on to read. Rachel was, she knew, slightly less patient with her own children, having been unable to shake off the vibe of the workday. One night, a few glasses into the wine bottle, she poured out her feelings to her husband. "I know I can do this job," she told him. "I think I can be a good manager. But I don't like the manager I'm becoming right now. I'm not sure this promotion was worth it."

Sometimes we're not quite able to put a finger on why we come home from work grumpy when nothing obvious has gone wrong that day. We're just not centered or happy. What we don't realize is that subtle challenges to our identity through personal and professional relationships pile up on us invisibly from day to day and week to week. Maybe you respond to your own pressure by passing it on to someone on your team despite knowing that they're struggling to keep up. You don't feel good about doing that, but, feeling pressure yourself, you cave. Or maybe you go along with the decision to pass over someone for a promotion because they're out of political favor, even though you know they really deserve that promotion. Because challenges to our identity come at us in an unending stream of small moments, we may not pause to register what each decision is doing to us. But we know we don't feel quite right.

Microstresses that challenge our identity are harder to spot than those that drain either our capacity or our emotional reserves. Capacity-draining microstresses are obvious once you pause to look for them, as are emotion-draining microstresses, which can become clear once you uncover why you're feeling exhausted or drained after certain interactions. They are built up, slowly, in the interactions we've come to accept as normal at work or in our personal lives because the people and environment around us accept them as normal. Many of the people we interviewed shared with us how interactions at work had slowly caused them to shift their values in small steps, as happened with Rachel, until suddenly, when they stopped to look, they didn't quite recognize who they were anymore. They were just different somehow. This was particularly acute for people whose sense of identity revolves around work. When work is the primary way we identify who we are and what our value is to the world, we can find ourselves simply "going along" with pushes and pulls to our self-identity because we're part of something larger. But that can also easily pull us into being someone we don't want to be. As one interviewee told us, "I've become one of those people I never used to like. I don't even know how this happened."

Throughout our interviews, we consistently heard many successful people describe stark moments in their lives when they finally grasped that they had just spent three, five, or even ten years in pursuit of things that conflicted with who they wanted to be when they started their careers. Their wake-up moments were often heartbreaking to hear. One woman told us that she thought her work colleagues were real friends until none of them checked in with her when she had a rough case of Covid-19, even though they knew she lived alone. When she emailed all her colleagues to say she was really struggling, not a single person asked how they could help. Another man told us that he realized at a parent-teacher night that his teenage son had no idea what he did at a global investment bank. The student described his dad as a "robber baron" to his history teacher. The father realized that he seldom talked about work in positive ways—not because his work was too complicated to explain but because he wasn't particularly proud of what he was contributing to the world.

On reflection, many interviewees came to understand that years of small choices led to that one wake-up moment. And those who had these epiphanies were the lucky ones. Many people never saw how their lives had become inconsistent with values and an identity they once held dear. In fact, an all-too-common theme in our interviews was how a conventionally successful person who had risen to the heights of their professional world but had left in their wake one or more divorces, children they felt totally disconnected from, and health teetering on disaster. The microstresses that challenged these people's identities had led them down a path they never intended, one small decision at a time.

Experiences and relationships outside of work can also result in shifts in our values as our lives evolve. We see how others measure success through social status and possessions, so we start using those metrics, too. These social comparisons occur rapidly, often beneath our awareness. They create a sense of dissatisfaction with what we have in life and lead us to pursue material wealth in ways that challenge our values. We unwittingly absorb other people's definition of success. And there can be a terrible price to pay for that. As you're reading this, we're sure you can think of someone whose life you think has gone horribly wrong because they've focused on the wrong things. The interviewees in our research often spoke of their mistake of taking "one step too far," in which they pushed themselves to stretch to a fancier house or took a job that required much more time on the road at the expense of their family to keep up with what they thought were expectations of success. But that version of success never quite felt right.

Because identity-challenging microstresses are the hardest to spot, you have to be attuned to their subtle signs. We can perhaps best describe it as an uncomfortable feeling when you're asked to do something that makes you feel slightly offbalance. *I don't like what that person is asking of me, but it's just a small thing, so I'll go along.* Or *I feel a little bad that I missed my daughter's math tournament, but I'll get to the next one.* We're not talking here about pressure to be deceptive, underhanded, or, God forbid, act illegally. Microstresses that challenge your identity are far more imperceptible. There's a vague discomfort with the choices you are making—however you justify them in your mind.

Microstresses That Challenge Your Identity

Identifying the microstresses that might be challenging our identity or values can be tricky because they probably have built up slowly, over time. We often just accept them, one by one, as part and parcel of our job or increased responsibilities at home. But once we identify them, we can begin to push back by reshaping our interactions and relationships to better support being the person we set out to be. Let's look at four common sources of microstress that challenge our identity by sneaking into our everyday life.

Microstress 11: Subtle Conflict with Your Personal Values

It's easy to draw a line when you're faced with choices that clearly feel wrong. But microstresses challenge your values in less obvious ways. First, the interactions tend to be everyday ones, smaller, or reasonably low stakes. Someone asks you to cut corners on a project to bring things in on time or under budget, despite the subpar quality. Second, they may be more complicated interactions where complexity and control are not clear. Your company might do business with a client whose organization harms the environment, manufacturers parts used in weapons, or is led by a controversial CEO. Or perhaps you don't share some of your organization's values—you care deeply about your direct reports, but your organization seems far less committed to developing their careers.

None of these things has a direct impact on you, at least on the surface, but these microstresses can sear into your soul. Even if you feel uncomfortable with a decision, you may feel compelled to go along because people around you are passionate about it and their zeal drives you into pursuits and interactions that don't feel quite right. This disconnect between your values and your actions frequently happens, for example, when people are part of collaborative sales efforts like banking, software, or consulting, where expectations can be oversold. There's a mismatch between what was sold and what the client received, leaving those involved to deal with negative interactions downstream as the client discovers and is less than thrilled with the outcome.

But even beyond these direct impacts, conflicts with personal values can also produce secondary effects that come back to us through relationships. Some of the secondary effects, such as reduced passion for work and taking our microstress home with us, are the same as for other microstresses. But one effect is unique to microstresses that challenge our identity: the feeling of being trapped.

Why You End Up Feeling Trapped

A real cognitive dissonance emerges when a career is going well and yet you feel stuck. It's not an easy problem to fix. Part of you justifies the ways that your job feels inconsistent with your personal values because it's worth the payoff to provide for your family and you'd lose so much if you walked away. You may lose seniority, the internal network you've worked hard to build, and the trust you've earned in your current job. So, you feel compelled to ignore the firm's actions that clash with your values. Again, we're not referring to ignoring rank corruption or legally questionable acts. These microstresses are far less obvious. It may bother you that the company doesn't provide employees with adequate mental health benefits, or you may feel that your company doesn't treat its hourly workers with enough respect. Sticking with a job that benefits you and your family at the expense of others can undermine your life satisfaction through a constant barrage of microstresses.

Consider what happened to Leslie, a regional manager at a major retail chain. She was responsible for nearly 20 percent of the company's brick-and-mortar stores in the United States. Those stores provided employment for thousands of people and gave millions of customers access to affordable, quality goods. But the company prided itself on its aggressive cost management, which sometimes resulted in what Leslie considered less-than-admirable actions toward employees and suppliers. The company had a stingy maternity policy. Suppliers were given harsh business terms and terminated with penalties if they failed to meet them, no matter the reason. To cope with her discomfort with policies like this, Leslie had grown increasingly transactional in her work as she climbed the corporate ladder. She didn't want to care too much about the people around her. Her energy and enthusiasm for the job had waned, and it seemed to her that the people around her were increasingly becoming transactional, too. She and her colleagues got work done together, but she rarely had a connection with anyone beyond that.

But Leslie had a moment of insight as she and her husband watched New Year's Eve fireworks over the harbor in Amsterdam one year. With their kids grown and gone, they had decided to treat themselves to a three-week European vacation. Removed from the everyday stresses of her job and thinking about her New Year's goals and resolutions, Leslie recognized why she'd become so disengaged. One of her first bosses at the company had told her years ago, "We are in business to provide our shareholders a return on their investment; that's the bottom line of everything we do." As she thought about what goals she'd focus on in the next year, she realized that forbidding herself to care about the people she worked with had left a void in her life. It wasn't who she wanted to be. "I kept thinking about something my mother had said to me years ago," she told us. "'Think about what you want your eulogy to be like someday. Do you want them to say you were great at helping your company make money? Or do you want them to say you made the world a little bit better?'"

A Realistic Path Forward

Once she saw how the values disconnect affected her, Leslie began to construct what she called a life revitalization plan. On the plane back from Europe, she made a list of the values that were important to her personally. Then she split her list into three—values that she could enact at work, values that she could enact outside work, and values that didn't seem possible in her life at the time.

Leslie was realistic about what was feasible. "I didn't have a 'Jerry McGuire' moment," she told us, referring to the movie in which the character Tom Cruise plays has an attack of conscience and writes a new manifesto for the company in which profit is no longer the primary motivation. "But I did try to find small ways I could make my world a better place." Over the next few months, she helped initiate a mentoring program for groups that were underrepresented in the current management structure, and she persuaded the executive committee to support a trial project to turn obsolete inventory into funds to support local food banks. She also began to work with her regional managers to champion product sourcing that was more responsible. She had presented these initiatives to her manager in a way that demonstrated they would not cost money and could benefit the company intangibly. Not least, she told him, the initiatives would be meaningful interactions to her.

"A year later," she said, "I wake up every morning eager to get to work. Sure, the company still did things that I didn't personally approve of, but you have to pick your battles. My new initiatives helped me do that, and they also energized and inspired my direct reports and even some of my peers."

We're not suggesting that you should have an epiphany about your identity and dramatically change everything overnight. There's too much at stake for many of us—and those who rely on us—to do that. However, we did find that many of the interviewees, like Leslie, were able to make a few small changes that had a significant impact on their sense of self, both at work and at home. But you have to recognize how microstresses that challenge your identity can eat away at you, and then you must decide not to settle for that.

Strategies for Pushing Back on Microstresses That Challenge Your Personal Values

Challenges to your identity can creep into your life very subtly. But once you're aware that they are happening, you can find effective ways to counter them.

Develop and Maintain Clarity on Your Personal Priorities

You may currently be in a job that doesn't perfectly fit with your values, but you can still find ways to make elements of it work better for you. Start by reflecting on these three questions:

- What expertise do you want to employ in your work over the next five to ten years?

- What values do you want to experience and live through this work?

- What identity do you want to shape through your professional role?

Just because your current job doesn't perfectly align with your answers doesn't mean you can't find moments in your day or create experiences at work that will bring you closer in line with what is meaningful to you. Look for a mentor who has the expertise you seek. Develop relationships with colleagues who seem to share your values. Craft a development plan to gain these experiences, even if you must seek out extra opportunities or projects at work. A temporary surge in workload may be worth it in the long term if it leads to your developing future opportunities around the work you find meaningful. And the more you lean in, the more your work role begins to align with values. Do the same for your personal life, writing down the roles you want to play that are important to you—athlete, friend, provider, social-justice warrior, musician or artist, and so on. Throughout our research, it was incredibly clear that our happiest people had much more granular clarity on the expertise they wanted to develop and the values they wanted to live. In contrast, ambiguity on these issues almost always led to situations where people were shaped by—rather than shaping—the system they were in.

Create Rituals That Help You Assess How You're Doing against Your Aspirations

Your periodic self-assessments might involve weekly journaling, a monthly discussion with your partner, or a quarterly check-in on the things you identified as important in both your personal and professional life. One person in our research set time aside once a month with their spouse and children to review family values, share past activities that reflected those values, and discuss areas where they were struggling. Whatever approach you use, assess your progress, target any actions that can close the gaps you find, and modify your goals as needed. Ideally, do this with those you're most interdependent with in life—your partner and maybe children, too—to create a mutually reinforcing system.

Recognize That You Can't Live Your Values 100 Percent Every Day

There will surely be times when you don't agree with what's happening in your organization, but sometimes that's just life. Decide what's important to fight for, and do your best to connect with work, clients, and leaders who support your values. When there's a disconnect with values, you'll need to decide how important it is for you to resolve the conflict.

One manager we spoke with told us, "I always want to be part of the solution. I will accept frustration and personal sacrifice to make things better for those who are going to come after me, and the junior people I work with, because at the end of the day, I think my ability to impact other people is all that really matters." But you only have a limited number of chips to play, and you must decide where you'll use your political capital; if you fight for everything, you eventually lose credibility.

Microstress 12: Undermined Confidence

Even if you haven't explicitly identified your values, you can figure out what they are in part by the things you take pride in being good at. Microstress undermines your ability to do that. "I started my career excited about being deeply respected for what I do professionally," one leader told us. "But this role is so overwhelming now that all I do is make decisions on what balls to drop—not how to be great."

The microstresses that undermine your confidence don't have to come from a single person, say, a boss who places unreasonable expectations on you. Rather, they more typically arise from the demands of work in this hyperconnected world. Confidence can be shaken in small ways, such as when role design or performance-management systems make it feel almost impossible to succeed. It can happen when you're embedded in overly inclusive cultures, where the sheer number of people who need to be involved in any decision makes it difficult to move anything forward. Or you're being pulled in so many directions that you give up pursuit of what is best or right and fall back to just getting through. Even though you believe you are a conscientious, innovative team player or good leader (and so on), your performance doesn't reflect those characteristics. You end up feeling like a failure, even though you're not the one creating the disconnect.

There are also damaging downstream effects of regularly having your self-confidence or control undermined. You may begin to work in ways that backfire, because you're so focused on avoiding making a mistake. Here are two common downstream effects of damaged self-confidence.

WORKING DEFENSIVELY. When we repeatedly feel that our competence at work is challenged, it's easy to take a more passive posture, attempting to preempt criticism rather than doing our best work. We focus less on the best ideas or right course of action and focus on avoiding problems.

This defensive approach backfires because we're no longer seen as high-potential or creative employees by our peers and managers.

REINFORCING A VICTIM MENTALITY. When we feel we are falling short of who we want to be at work, we can find ourselves blaming others because we see ourselves as victims, unappreciated and unfairly treated by colleagues. Then we talk with our close family and friends about the microstress slights and insults we experienced at work, and they try to support us. But since they only know what we tell them (and let's face it, we often tell them what happened in ways designed to generate maximum sympathy), our loved ones can end up reinforcing our growing victim mentality: "Your boss is being totally unreasonable!" It might feel good hearing that in the moment, but with this validation, our feelings of victimhood can build up until we're ready to explode. So what started as empathy can spiral into something that triggers you to the situation rather than ever trying to improve it.

. . .

Consider the experience of Ali, an HR rep at a major telecom. He was excited to be promoted into a new role that required him to manage high-profile projects. But as he tried to bring his very best to his job, little by little his confidence was crushed by his manager. Ali's boss seemed to subtly undermine him. For example, after Ali had invested weeks in an external talent search to fill a new role, he was surprised to learn in a passing conversation that his boss had casually suggested to the team that they abandon the search and hire an internal candidate instead. Ali didn't know about the decision until after it was made. He heard about it from the person he was supposed to be working *with*. "She's going to think my boss doesn't trust me," he worried. "And now I kind of look like a fool for not knowing what was going on. Here I am, talking enthusiastically to outside candidates about a job that's already been filled."

After several such incidents, Ali began to lose his enthusiasm for pushing ahead on big projects, something he felt he was good at. "Why should

I bother killing myself when it's going to be trashed eventually anyway?" he thought. He started doubting his own judgment. He tried to think about what his boss would do, rather than use his own judgment to make suggestions.

Eventually, Ali started to look around outside the firm for a new position. In the process, he asked an old friend who had been his manager ten years earlier whether she would be willing to be a reference for him in his job search. "Of course," she said. "But you're in such a great position now. Why are you thinking of quitting?" Ali poured out his heart to her, describing how he felt he was being undermined by his boss, whom she knew. "Would you allow me to reach out to him to see if I can get a sense of what's going on?" she offered. Feeling as though he had little to lose, Ali agreed, on the condition that she be discreet about the fact that Ali was looking to jump ship.

A week later, she reconnected with Ali. She had spoken with his boss to try to understand the dynamic. In their conversation, the friend had learned that Ali's quiet and unassuming style had been completely misinterpreted by his boss. Ali's boss liked him, but he was never sure if Ali was on top of his assignments. Wanting to shore him up, the boss thought he was helping by offering his experience and stepping in with clients. Where Ali was disheartened by his boss's intervention, the boss thought he was providing advocacy and support. The truth probably lay somewhere between the two extremes, but without someone to help reconcile the two experiences, Ali and his boss would never have realized what was going on. And Ali most likely would have quit, never knowing that his boss thought he was helping him succeed.

Having even that small insight into his boss's perspective gave Ali the courage to engage differently with him. He now started every conversation with his boss by reviewing the facts of the situation before laying out what he saw as the options. He also began to see his boss as a resource rather than a micromanager. Securing his boss's input early gave Ali the support to proceed down the right path and assure his boss that Ali was on top of his work and could be trusted. It was a subtle but effective change. And one that helped Ali begin to thrive in his new job.

A year after Ali had been ready to quit, his boss had given him ever-increasing decision authority without Ali needing to always check in. They still collaborated on big things, but they had created a mentoring relationship intended to build skills that Ali didn't yet have rather than a remedial supervisory relationship.

Strategies for Pushing Back on Microstresses That Undermine Your Confidence

People around us can rattle our confidence in small moments—often in ways that they're not even aware of. Unchecked, these chips at your confidence can undermine your day, your week, or even more. But you can stop those microstress moments from sending you reeling.

Tackle the Problem Head-On by Directly Engaging the Person

If someone is a common source of microstresses that undermine your confidence, make a point of asking questions that will help you understand their primary objectives and pain points. See things from their perspective. Then, do all you can to help them along one or more of the tracks that matter to them. As you become increasingly helpful, their aggressive tendencies will often diminish in ways that direct combat with more facts and figures or logic can't accomplish. Over time, the narrative around you will change as this person sees you as an active supporter and problem-solver.

Approach the Problem Indirectly, through Your Network

If someone you trust has influence with the person causing you microstress, see whether this ally might feel comfortable pointing out to the other person what's happening in an unbiased and nonconfrontational way. Keeping the issue out of the public light in this way may reduce the other person's defensiveness, and hearing it from a neutral third party might make them gain insight into their own behavior.

Add Structure to Conversations to Keep Them Productive

Suggest that meetings follow basic ground rules to help separate substantive issues from personality clashes. Focus on the facts, compare multiple alternatives, identify common goals, use humor, balance the power structure, and seek consensus but defer to authority. If you aren't in a position to do this, perhaps engage a facilitator who could help people identify when they're being too critical and help everyone separate out concerns about an idea from personal criticism.

Microstress 13: Draining or Other Negative Interactions with Family or Friends

Ever show up at work not feeling good about yourself because you snapped at your partner in the rush to get out of the house? The clash can throw off your whole day. Or perhaps a simple text from your child while you're at work—"My teacher says he won't help me with my history essay and it's due tomorrow"—can spin into hours of worry. Is your child not living up to the teacher's expectations? Being lazy? Is the teacher being a jerk? Is your child struggling? And so on. But in reality, your text-happy child might have been simply blowing off steam momentarily. By the time you finally catch up with them in person, they've long since forgotten what they texted you, while you've been anxious about it for hours. You spend your day distracted, worrying about what's wrong, imagining worst-case scenarios, until you get home and see that everything's fine. We can get wrapped up in a loved one's problem when we need to step in and mediate (perhaps among family members or with your child's teacher), and suddenly their microstress is ours, too. And because of often-unrealistic societal and cultural expectations about what makes a good parent, a good partner, a good sibling, a good child, and a good friend, many of us are plagued with constant guilt for how we handle these situations.

For many people, their friends and family are the most significant sources of unrecognized microstress. We're not talking about toxic relationships with estranged relatives or outright hostile exchanges with a former friend. Instead, we're talking about the minor, everyday inter-actions with people we care about most—the interactions that leave us drained long afterward. Passive-aggressive exchanges with a sibling over who is hosting a holiday dinner. A tense conversation with a longtime friend who has new political views you don't agree with. The wound you nurse when a passing comment from your own parent suggests they don't approve of some small choice you've made in your life. Microstresses that come from family and friends pose a special form of stress because they concern lifelong relationships often embedded within complicated friend-ship or family dynamics. Because we love these people or at least share a history with them, our emotional reaction to microstresses in those relationships is magnified. We can't simply walk away from an interac-tion that goes badly.

And that's just the direct impact of the microstress. Microstress cre-ated by difficult interactions with family and friends compounds over time in a variety of ways.

SNOWBALLING DISPUTES. A difficult interaction with a family member can spill over into your broader social network. You may have found yourself at political odds with your Uncle Frank, and perhaps other family members have become uncomfortable having both of you at events, so you stop getting invited. You may overshare some temporary frustrations about your sibling at the dinner table, and your own children start to distance themselves from a once-beloved aunt because they sense there's a family feud brewing. Stories about negative interactions can take on a life of their own and circulate among people who then judge us poorly, which in turn creates further stress. You end up thinking you have to manage the ripple effects that you unintentionally set in motion, fueling your microstress even more.

TAKING OUR HOME LIFE TO WORK. Just as we often take work stress home with us, stresses from our personal lives can spill over into our work lives, sucking up time, interrupting work routines, and distracting us from important priorities. We might have to rush out of work to tend to something. We cut corners on the day but worry that our colleagues are starting to think we don't pull our weight. Or we spend too much time in a work meeting talking about a family struggle when our colleagues only wanted quick pleasantries. Then, in a vicious cycle, when we become less effective at work, the resulting stress spills back over into our home life.

FEELINGS OF FAMILIAL FAILURE. In some ways, this is the most debilitating microstress that challenges your identity. Even though we intellectually know that expectations about what constitutes good behavior in a family role can be unrealistic, we still worry that we're falling short for the people we love most. In our minds, we are not the spouse, partner, sibling, or child that our loved ones deserve. Even if we're already doing a lot, the guilt that comes from thinking we're never doing enough compounds our microstress.

Strategies for Pushing Back on Draining Interactions with Family and Friends

The relationships that are most important in your life are often the ones most fraught with stress. So start by getting the basics right.

Align Your Family on Priorities, Life Goals, and Where You Invest Your Time and Money

Start with your anchor relationships: make sure you have regular conversations, make trade-offs together, and be clear on what outcomes are important to all of you and what can be sacrificed. For example, one interviewee had a quarterly alignment conversation with his wife to see if they agreed on their priorities and how they had each been spending their time and energy. Another couple created lighthearted report cards that they discussed each month on date night. Though the feedback was given kindly or in jest, it was enough to spur good conversations about what they could be doing better.

Engage your children in similar conversations to ensure that everyone feels part of the team. Ask them how you're doing as a parent! The interaction doesn't have to be an intense conversation; it can just be a quick check-in. If you don't know that an issue is brewing, you cannot deal with it. Planning regularly in this way can prevent negativity from arising.

Have Candid, Forwarding-Looking Conversations to Address Issues

Some of the people we interviewed made subtle shifts in their interactions with others to minimize the microstress in small ways. Consider how Mila, a department manager in a global software company, coped with the increasingly stressful challenges of coordinating the care for her aging parents with her siblings. A single phone call at work from her sister to schedule a medical appointment for their dad could affect her whole day.

"I wasn't very nice," she confessed. "The only thing I could think about was whether I was going to have to take off yet another day from work, and I was snippy with her." Because Mila worked full time, her sister ended up shouldering more responsibility for the day-to-day needs of their parents. And Mila felt guilty about that. She and her sister never openly fought, but things inevitably got tense whenever they walked through whatever new need had arisen. "I just ended up feeling bad about myself, no matter what we decided," Mila said.

Fortunately, rather than immediately booking another day off from work, Mila took a step back and recognized that she and her sister were making reactive decisions rather than putting together a plan for how to handle their parents' increasing needs. So, she suggested that they have dinner to talk about how the future might need to go. Each of them shared how they felt like they were falling short—not just with their parents but with their own families. "I had no idea how she was feeling," Mila told us. "I thought she was just disappointed in me. It was really helpful to have such a candid conversation." Both of them also voiced for the first time their frustration that they routinely stepped up to help their parents but that somehow their brother never did. He had a busy job as managing partner of a consulting firm, but the sisters never even considered asking for his help. They hated how they had fallen into gender stereotypes that suggest that women in the family are always the ones who step up for extra family needs. That wasn't how they thought of their family dynamic, and they certainly didn't want their own children to pick up on that message.

So Mila and her sister instituted routine scheduling conversations every couple of weeks to walk through what they knew was coming up. The conversation then would be focused on planning, rather than subtly implying that one or the other was doing more than her share. They asked their brother to help out on weekends, for example, when he wasn't busy at work. To their surprise, he was happy to step up. He had felt isolated from the decisions they were making without his input about their parents' care and was glad to finally be part of the conversation. And they all agreed that they couldn't handle the situation alone indefinitely. They asked their brother to explore resources they could use from the senior citizens council in their parents' hometown.

By stepping back and examining the destructive patterns that she and her siblings were falling into, Mila was able to reshape how and when they worked together to assist their parents without spiraling into anger at one another.

Change How You Deal with Negative People

Consider the broad set of interactions you have with each important person in your life and how you might alter each relationship. You might try to change a behavior or distance yourself from a person by delaying responses or just seeing them on holidays. Or you might be brave enough to remove yourself from relationships that are persistently destructive.

You probably have someone in your life like this. Perhaps it's an extended family member who always sees the worst in everything. Even small interactions with them can leave you rattled. You don't have to immediately cut that person out of your life, but you can find ways to limit your contact. Do this by decreasing the number of interactions each year, limiting your own availability during visits (don't sit next to them at the family holiday table), and ensure that when you do meet, it's in a large group of people so that their negativity can be tempered by the crowd. But if these efforts don't remove the microstress from your life with this person, consider making a bigger change. Even though separating entirely from someone runs counter to society's messages of having to be a good friend or family member, many interviewees found that sometimes the best solution is to do just that.

Accept That Some Things Are beyond Your Control

Put limits on what you're willing to do, and then give yourself permission to ignore the rest. Talk to people who are in similar situations to get a sense of what's reasonable and what isn't. The conversation may also reassure you that some things are just hard and that you're not alone in these struggles. One person we interviewed encountered significant stress through a conflict with school officials who tried to remove her developmentally delayed son from the school. After an extended battle to keep her son in the school, she joined a support group for parents of kids with similar issues. She found out that if she did withdraw him, she would be on her own in figuring out his education. Instead, she followed the other parents' advice and refused the withdrawal, appealing to school-board leadership to transfer her boy to a school that could provide him with the support he needed.

Microstress 14: Disruptions to Your Network

Our triumphs, failures, and resilience are almost always shaped by the people who are with us during that time. They become an integral part of our sense of who we are. We may look back fondly on really challenging times at work, because we had deep respect for our colleagues: we were in this together. Or we may count on people in our personal life to help keep us strong during difficult life challenges. Our sense of who we are in the world is shaped in significant ways by the people and groups with whom we interact. So, when our connection to these people is disrupted— sometimes for no fault of our own—we feel it deeply.

Many of us have been fortunate to have genuine friendships in our working lives. Not surprisingly, when a close colleague or terrific boss leaves, we feel a bit lost. Overnight, we lose an extension of ourselves— someone who not only helped us to get work done but also helped us endure workplace microstresses. We have to find new ways to collaborate with people we haven't previously connected with. We must reposition ourselves with others, trying to build trust when we haven't previously had to worry about that. Or when we start a new role, even if it's in the same company, we become the new kid all over again. We have to learn how things get done, who matters, and how to interpret the political landscape. And we experience greater stress, partly because we have lost the people who had become our allies, helping us make sense of things, supported our efforts, and cared about the same things we did. Without those people to counterbalance the battering of microstress in our every-day lives, we can find ourselves less insulated from the stresses around us.

Other follow-on stresses are also likely.

RIPPLE EFFECTS FOR FAMILY. Any parent who has ever relocated for a job knows how hard it is to extricate the kids from their settled lives and thrust them into a new one. Such a move is undoubtedly a major stress. But it also comes wrapped in invisible layers of microstress. Your children have to figure out new neighborhood norms, find the courage to walk into the local teen center alone, or establish themselves at an unfamiliar dance class. Everyone in your family may have to change medical providers, starting from scratch with each one, after years spent building relationships with your previous doctors. You and your partner may have decided to move together, but that doesn't mean your partner won't be hit by waves of microstress. They may have left behind friends and other important social outlets. Of course, these microstresses all boomerang back on us—the stresses our loved ones feel as their networks are shifted affect us, and vice versa.

THE TOLL OF REBUILDING. Even minor shifts in our lives can trigger the need to rebuild our networks of allies, advisers, and supporters. Say you move departments at work. Your new department has a different rhythm, different norms. You might not be able to plan on Friday lunches with your pals in other parts of the company anymore. Figuring out the new lay of the land takes effort and an investment of time that can take you away from your primary obligations. Maybe you can't cut out early on Thursdays for your guitar lesson, as you used to. You have to figure out which colleagues will have your back if you struggle to get up to speed on something. You often consequently face the stress of having to work twice as hard to do well in your job while you're rebuilding networks.

FADING CONNECTIONS. For many of us, the demands of work and life eat away at our ability to stay connected with groups that had been a powerful antidote to the microstresses of everyday life. We don't mean for this to happen; our connections just erode over time. We fall out of athletic groups we once enjoyed, disappear from spiritual pursuits, or lose our social connections because we're focusing on work. But without the counterbalance of these nonwork networks, we experience more deeply— and react more poorly to—the everyday microstresses in our lives.

. . .

Just because a change might be positive doesn't make it easy. For example, Carlton, a leader in a large industrial organization, shared how he found himself feeling unexpectedly adrift when his company was acquired by a global giant. The acquisition brought a battery of positive changes, including a bump in his salary and seniority to level him up to his peers elsewhere in the organization. And even though his work life was not much different on paper—he was still a midlevel manager in the same department with a handful of direct reports—Carlton felt as if he were starting from scratch. He had to figure out where he fit in, who he could join forces with, where the minefields were, and what the opportunities were. Everyone was pleasant enough, but he couldn't help but feel isolated from his new colleagues, many of whom had known one another for years.

His buddy Scott in finance, who had always cut him slack on late expense reports, had been shifted to a different role in the new organization. And in this new structure, Carlton reported up to a veteran manager from the global company. This manager didn't seem to have the time to get to know Carlton beyond their functional interactions. Carlton explained: "My previous manager, Susan, was so good at talking me off the ledge when I felt overwhelmed with work. But she left the company after the merger. Now I'm afraid to let my new manager know when I'm feeling that way, because he might think I'm not up for the job." He worried that his new colleagues might sense his anxiety and assume he lacked self-confidence.

Fortunately, as he approached the one-year mark in his new job, he seized on a moment to connect with one of his new peers in a different office. While he and the person who ran logistics for his facility were discussing routine matters, the colleague mentioned a minor supply-chain problem in passing. Carlton's ears pricked up: it sounded similar to an issue that he had been instrumental in solving at his company before the merger. After asking a few more questions to explore the problem and confirm that he understood it, Carlton offered to help solve it. Playing any role in the supply chain issue was not part of his job, but he knew he could be helpful. And more important, he saw a chance to connect with his colleague in a completely different way from their previously purely functional conversations. Within two months, Carlton had helped make the problem virtually disappear. And more important, he'd made an ally.

Carlton learned that trying to use his experience to help his new colleagues could be a powerful relationship builder. So he made a point of reaching out to colleagues in other parts of the company, ostensibly to discuss some joint matter. But he would make sure that each of these conversations gave him a chance to ask them questions. "Hey, I'm still trying to understand how things work with our parent company," he would ask. "I'd love if you would share with me what you are trying to accomplish but are struggling with." Though some conversations went nowhere and others revealed issues Carlton couldn't help with, some discussions uncovered things that he was in a good position to assist with. When he saw an opportunity, Carlton leaned into helping resolve those problems. Even when he didn't identify an issue, he used those meetings to drift off topic and onto personal matters. Even simply asking "What are you up to this weekend?" or "Do you have any interesting trips planned?" occasionally yielded common interests. In the process, he found a new wine aficionado, someone who shared his passion for golf, and a fellow biking enthusiast.

Two years after the merger, Carlton's workplace network included a range of friends and allies, including several senior leaders who have helped him find his place in the company.

Strategies to Navigate Disruptions to Your Network

Your own success in a transition—large or small—will depend on creating connections and good will with a wide range of people. Connect with key stakeholders, customers, and clients, and create new networks of friends and connections outside of work.

Lean into Transitions

Transitions are not easy, even in the best circumstances. So proactively initiate transitions into groups—such as a new role, job, or community—when things are going well. Expanding your networks will help ensure that you don't rely too heavily on any one source of identity. Rebuilding a network from scratch is hard, especially on the personal side. One person we interviewed tried to ensure that his transition into a new job would not be difficult for his family by limiting his job search to opportunities in his current firm or in other organizations in a city his family had

COACHING BREAK

Understanding What You Value

You can't push back on challenges to your identity if you lack a clear grasp of who you are and what you value. Here are three steps you can follow to begin to capture your own thoughts.

1. Identify Your Core Values

Start by creating a chart with the first column for your core values and the remaining four columns for microstresses threatening those values. (Table 4-1 shows how one high performer conducted this exercise.) In the first column, identify three professional and three personal values. Be specific. On a professional level, these might entail mentoring, creativity, sustainability, social justice, growing a business, making a lot of money, co-creating a desired future with work colleagues, or having a positive or life-changing impact on a client. On a personal level, your values might include community involvement, helping people who are underprivileged, showing up for family, and being a good friend. Try to recall stretches of your life where you were thriving, and think carefully about how the values and interactions you had with others created these times.

2. Identify the Forces Pulling You Away from Those Values

Identify the microstress that might be pulling you from this version of yourself. Be precise in the negative interactions that are keeping you from being that person. (Remember, negative interactions always have far greater impact on your life satisfaction than do positive ones).

TABLE 4-1

What do you value?

Core value	Microstresses pushing against your core values		
	Pressure to pursue goals out of sync with your personal values	When someone undermines your self-confidence, worth, or control	Disruptions to your network	Negative/draining interactions with family and friends
Professional				
To become a deep expert in data science	Pressure from direct leader to take shortcuts on analytics to increase number of projects completed	Uncoordinated requests coming from different stakeholders with insufficient time to do role well		
To be a servant leader concerned with others' development and success	Pressure from leader to minimize cost structure precludes development opportunities		Departures of core allies in functional groups makes securing additional resources for team harder	
To be a positive source of energy and inspiration for others at work			Closest work colleague left company for pursuit of other opportunity, removing key relationship that used to reenergize you in small moments	Interactions with struggling teen affecting the energy remaining for work colleagues
Personal				
To live spiritual values through service and relationships at church		Excessive work demands from disconnected stakeholders driving work into times used to spend with groups from church	Recent breakup of core group that you had been a part of for six years; relationships feel less anchored to church	
To be a devoted spouse	Tough boss creating work demands that are taking quality time away from relationship with spouse			Difficulty with teenage child taking time that you would otherwise devote to spouse
To actively contribute to making the world a better place		Erratic workload due to role design resulting in missed volunteering at English as a second language group and food pantry volunteering		

(continued)

3. Make a Plan to Shift Negative Interactions

Identify three specific actions you will take to address the most consequential microstresses in the chart you are completing. Common steps include speaking with the person or people with whom you've had negative exchanges to alter your interactions; approaching someone these people trust and listen to, to convey your message if a direct approach is too difficult; increasing the time between your interactions; or shortening their duration. And if all else fails, you can always remove yourself from the interaction. One high performer we interviewed came up with this list of actions:

- Create gating function and time estimates for work coming into team to prioritize and set boundaries.

- Engage boss in discussion to align on development needs and benefits for team.

- Sit down with full family to agree on core values important to us and how we can ensure that each member is fulfilled.

---

enjoyed living in five years earlier. When he found a new job in that city, he and his spouse bought a home around the corner from where they used to live. His wife rejoined her old a cappella group. In this way, they preemptively mitigated some of the inevitable microstresses that accompanied such a move.

Avoid the Trap of Narrow Focus in a Transition

When you're moving into a new situation—a change in job, a shift in the people working with you, or even a more major move—many people decide that they need to master what's new. To this end, they reduce their connections to people or activities that might distract them from their goal. But that is a mistake. Being too focused can lead to becoming unidimensional—you have few antidotes to the microstresses that are inevitably bombarding you at that time. So when things are tough at work (or at home) during such a transition, you have almost nothing else in your life to counterbalance the stress. Instead of staying laser focused, use a transition as the jumping-off point for building new networks to shape the work you want to do and whom you want to do it with. And use these transitions as times to reflect on the kinds of people you want to be part of your life outside work. Be intentional in building and revitalizing your circle of nonwork friends.

Reconnect with Your Past to Grow Your Network

Many people in their late thirties or their forties find that they have fallen out of activities and groups that used to be important to them. To counter this trend, rediscover your hobbies or passions from the past to slingshot yourself into new groups. One person we interviewed loved working on cars but for many years had had no time to pursue this interest. When his kids became teenagers, he bought a decrepit Ford Model A and started rebuilding it in his garage on Tuesday nights. Word spread, and for the next few years, his garage became a regular hangout for a half dozen middle-aged gearheads who helped him strip down the car, repair or replace broken parts, and share a beer.

Challenges to our identity don't always come at us in big fork-in-the-road moral decisions but can happen in everyday microstresses that erode our sense of self. Many of our interviewees described living for years in a kind of echo chamber, where the choices they made at work and in their personal lives were reinforced by the people around them, even when, with hindsight, those choices had put them on the wrong track. In our research, people who were on their second or even third marriages, who were unhealthy to the point of crisis, or who had estranged family relationships almost always had allowed life to become more one-dimensional or focused on what they believed others expected of them. These decisions came at them in microstresses, small moments that challenged their sense of self-identity along the way. Each individual choice made sense right up until it didn't. One interviewee told us how she had allowed her identity to be completely defined by her work for many years, something she hadn't fully realized until she hit a personal crisis. "My mother battled cancer and passed away after seven very difficult months," she told us. "No one from the company I had given eight hard years of my life to showed up at the funeral."

The microstresses that challenge your identity can take an insidious toll on your life—not least because you don't even realize what's happening. And the worst part is, you've been complicit in the process, making small, subtle decisions along the way, and these choices end up taking you far from the person you want to be. It's never too late to course correct, however. As we'll discuss in the next chapter, some of our high performers managed to avoid this trap. Though they are wildly successful professionally by anyone's definition, they have not allowed their success to cloud their sense of identity and values, both inside and outside of work. In fact, we believe they've achieved that success *because* they are so clear about who they are. Their life is defined by more than just their work. In the next chapter, we'll explore how they managed to strike this balance.

Chapter 5

What the Ten Percenters Get So Right

The ten percenters: *among the high performers we interviewed, the subset who are best in class at not only managing their microstress but also living rich, multidimensional lives through small moments of authentic connection with others*

 KEY INSIGHTS

- **Negative interactions always have disproportionately large impact on our well-being.** Eliminating even just two or three microstresses in your life can make a significant difference.

- **The ten percenters do three things well that the rest of us can learn from:**

  - Push back on individual microstresses
  - Recognize when they are causing microstresses that boomerang back on them
  - Live multidimensional lives that make many microstresses inconsequential to them

- **Other people are the reason we have microstress in our lives—but they're also part of the solution.** With subtle shifts in your habits and practices, you can find small ways to connect with other people in relationships that will not only provide a powerful antidote to microstress but also form a critical foundation of well-being through resilience, physical health, and purpose.

- **You don't need one or two ride-or-die friends to fight microstress.** Rather, a diversity of connections—at work and in your personal life—can help you keep your microstress in perspective. And help you build a more satisfying life.

- **The secret of ten percenters is that they live small moments more richly in connection with others.** They don't pursue happiness as something over the horizon they will someday reach—perhaps when they finally achieve a certain level of income or a particular job title or when they eventually retire. They structure their lives to create multiple groups they are an authentic part of. And they lean deeper into small moments of connection with others as key contributors to their resilience, physical well-being, and purpose.

What does half a million dollars mean to you?

It might sound like a fun what-if question, but Matthew had to answer the question for himself in real life. A company buyout meant that he would need to transfer to another city to keep his position and the lucrative salary and bonuses his job came with. It also set him up for growth—the fact that he was selected signaled that he was a high-potential employee with opportunities for rising even higher. At the same time, keeping his job would require uprooting his family. It would also mean leaving behind a large network of professional connections and a personal community he had developed—some friends were from his childhood. On the other hand, staying behind effectively meant leaving $500,000 in salary and bonuses on the table.

For the first time in his career, forty-three-year-old Matthew found himself paralyzed with indecision. His peers at work didn't understand his hesitation. How could he consider turning the opportunity down? Matthew described how people reacted: "Every single person in corporate life that I asked, within about thirty-five seconds, said, 'It's not even a decision, stupid! Why would you take a half-million-dollar pay cut?'"

After weeks of dithering, he finally decided to walk away from the position—and the half million dollars—in favor of a less lucrative job at a different company closer to home. His colleagues thought he was crazy. But Matthew has no regrets, except, he told us, that he had come so close to making the wrong choice.

Matthew was among the people we came to call the ten percenters, a name we give to the roughly one in ten of the people we interviewed. The ten percenters navigate the same volume and velocity of microstresses that others do, but this group manages to outperform other high performers at work while also maintaining happiness and meaning in their personal lives.

Matthew stood out because the vast majority of people we interviewed were struggling. As soon as you peeled back a layer or two, raw emotions came to the surface: exhaustion, guilt for letting people down, disappointment in family or friends, and a nagging sense of dissatisfaction with how their lives had turned out. And remember, these were the people who presumably had it all figured out—top performers in some of the world's most respected organizations. If they're struggling, what hope is there for the rest of us?

But now and again, an interview turned out differently. We'd come across a successful person who, like Matthew, was not beaten down. Who seemed to harbor few regrets. Who was physically healthier. Who had a rich life beyond work and family. The contrast was striking. These were the ten percenters, and we wanted to understand them and what they were doing differently.

Matthew and the other standouts in our research have little in common on the surface. They come from a variety of backgrounds, hold different positions in a variety of companies and industries. But we observed some recurring patterns. Each ten percenter has made deliberate choices to shape the relationships in their lives. They define success for themselves in a broad and multidimensional way, and they hold themselves accountable to it. Achieving that involves being connected to a wide variety of people, both in and out of work. And these connections, in turn, help them fend off crushing microstresses. It's a virtuous cycle.

In this chapter, we will explore the strategies the ten percenters use to mitigate microstress so that you can begin to apply them to your own life. We'll help you map out specific microstresses that you can alter, eliminate, or learn to accept. We'll help you recognize the microstress that you may be causing others. And then we'll explain how ten percenters preemptively protect themselves from the trauma of microstress by building and maintaining multidimensional lives filled with a variety of interests and relationships.

During our research, both of us began to adopt some of the ten percenters' practices. We can report that these efforts have made a meaningful difference to both of us personally and have increased our admiration of the ten percenters who seemed to live this way naturally. Here's what we can all learn from the ten percenters.

Get Your Microstress under Control

None of us can eliminate all microstress from our lives; doing so is unrealistic. But we can make things better. Research shows that negative interactions take a significant toll on all of us, carrying as much as five times the impact of positive ones. So, reducing even just a few microstresses in our lives can have a profound impact. We learned from our research that most people can find three to five opportunities to shift the effect of microstress in ways that will make a notable difference.

But with dozens of microstresses coming at you daily, how do you know where to begin? Do what the ten percenters do: think small. They have developed a sort of three-pronged approach to microstress that is highly effective:

- **Push back on specific microstresses in practical ways.** You can find small but effective ways to counter a handful of microstresses. Doing so will have an outsized impact in your daily life.

- **Stop causing microstress for others.** The "aha!" of this approach is that not only will it help others, but it will also help you. When you create microstress for others, the stress inevitably bounces back to you in one form or another. So triggering less microstress means you'll receive less microstress in return.

- **Rise above some microstresses.** One reason some microstresses affect us is simply that we let them. So much of our reaction is self-imposed; the more unidimensional we become in our lives, the more susceptible we are to overreaction. You can learn from the ten percenters how to live in ways that keep numerous microstresses in perspective.

Here's a simple exercise we developed to help you do just that. We've created a master chart of all the common categories of microstresses (table 5-1). The top row names the categories of people who might contribute to your microstress. The left-most column maps out where your microstress is coming from. This is a simple way to start to capture the forms of microstress that might be in your life.

First, identify two or three microstresses you can target to push back on. Pick those that have become systemic in your life—those that you have allowed to persist in your day-to-day struggles. Mark them with an X.

Think in small manageable units, not sweeping aspirational goals. Simply altering interactions, increasing time between the interactions, or, possibly, disconnecting in some way (which we will discuss later) can have a major impact on your overall well-being.

One executive told us that instead of vowing to turn off all text notifications during the workday—a practice that was not realistic—he asked his college-aged daughter not to text him with every passing complaint about her day. No longer would she blast him with inconsequential comments like "Professor Jones didn't laugh at my joke today" or "My roommate has been coming in after midnight every night, and I'm exhausted!" This one change eliminated an enormous amount of microstress for him. The mere act of texting her feelings to her dad helped the daughter resolve her stress almost immediately, but he would worry about her all day until he had a chance to speak to her. "A lot of times she wouldn't even remember what I was referring to," he said. "She'd forgotten it long ago, but I'd worry about it for hours, distracting me at work." Instead, he called her spontaneously when he was driving home from work. Sometimes she wasn't free to talk, but other times his call led to a wonderful stream-of-consciousness catch-up with her.

Next, take a second pass through the table, and reflect on two or three microstresses that you are creating for others. Place a large Y in those cells. You might need a few minutes to think this through, but we're certain you'll find some good examples of microstress you are creating. One executive told us he was so protective of his team that he found himself constantly hovering over their work, sometimes stepping in to answer for them in meetings, and frequently checking and questioning their work. This habit, he realized, was causing his team members to doubt their own skills. They would ask him a plethora of follow-up questions to make sure they were doing things his way, rather than stepping up to make decisions for themselves. The work they were doing was fine, certainly in the eyes of the client, but by setting the bar higher than it really needed to be, he had unintentionally made his team look weak in the eyes of their colleagues and he, in turn, looked like an ineffective manager.

Finally, in a third pass through the table, reflect on any microstresses that you are unnecessarily magnifying—interactions for which you need to learn to keep things in perspective a bit better. Place a large O in those cells. Most of us have had stretches in our lives when we are grumbling about all the microstresses we're facing, and then something genuinely traumatic happens—maybe a health issue, a death in the family, or the discovery that a loved one was dealing with a serious problem. In an instant, the things that seemed so important two minutes ago—a credit-stealing colleague, higher-ups who change their minds constantly, a simmering disagreement with your siblings—become insignificant in the grand scheme of things. We can all get too myopic about the microstresses in our lives. We obsess on things we can't change, spiraling into angry or bitter emotions that affect our work and our relationships. By actively selecting two or three of these microstresses to let go, you can stop being caught up in minutiae that does not matter in the long run. But you have to make a conscious choice to do that.

One of the people we interviewed told us that he was obsessed for years by the praise one of his peers seemed to be regularly offered by their manager. "It just got under my skin that she would be singled out in meetings for her work, and she'd be sitting there beaming like a Cheshire cat. I felt like there were politics at play that I had no chance of winning," he told us. As we probed, we learned that she hadn't been promoted ahead of him and she wasn't given more-favorable work assignments. He could rattle off a litany of small annoyances, but in reality, his own work wasn't affected by her at all. "I spend way too much time obsessing over something that doesn't actually affect my work very much," he concluded.

Let's walk through this exercise using the example of Melissa, as presented in table 5-1. Melissa was struggling to settle into a new job with a new manager and new colleagues. Experience told her that the stress would subside as she got used to her new boss and acclimated to her new peers. But months in, she still had not adjusted to her new situation. This exercise helped Melissa pinpoint what was going wrong and how she could address it.

For Melissa, one benefit of looking at her microstresses this way was the recognition of what she was dealing with daily. She knew that, realistically, she could not miraculously find a way to solve them all. Not that she didn't want to—she kept asking us if she could pick more than three priorities! The practical answer is no. But you can make an enormous difference if you focus your effort on a small set of microstresses that are both impactful and systematic enough that they warrant action. The key is to be very specific about what you want to change.

Melissa thought she was just stretched too thin between home and work and blamed herself for falling short. But through this exercise, she

TABLE 5-1

Identifying where your microstress is coming from

What is driving your stress?   **Who is driving your stress?**

	Boss	Leaders	Peers	Client	Team	Loved ones
MICROSTRESSES DRAINING YOUR PERSONAL CAPACITY						
Misalignment of roles or priorities						
Others' unreliability						
Unpredictable behavior from a person in authority	X					
Volume and diversity of collaborative demands					Y	
Surge in responsibilities at work or home						
MICROSTRESSES DEPLETING YOUR EMOTIONAL RESERVES						
Managing and feeling responsible for the success and well-being of others					X	
Confrontational conversations						
Mistrust in your network						
People who spread stress			Y		Y	
Political maneuvering			O			
MICROSTRESSES CHALLENGING YOUR IDENTITY						
Pressure to pursue goals out of sync with your personal values						
Attacks on your sense of self-confidence, worth, or control						
Draining or other negative interactions with family or friends	O					
Disruptions to your network						X

Note: X, microstresses targeted for action; Y, microstresses you are creating for others; O, microstresses that you are unnecessarily magnifying.

discovered that one specific source of microstress was a boss who was an unpredictable authority figure. This woman wasn't evil. She herself was trying to navigate the CEO's shifting priorities, which she passed on to Melissa. Microstress identified, Melissa was able to devise a strategy for pushing back. She started by asking her boss if they could prioritize her work together so that she'd be spending her time on the most important things. In their discussion, Melissa walked her boss through the impact of the boss's requests. She described two recent scenarios in depth: in one case, the boss's strategy shift meant that Melissa had to stop her team midstream on one project without making them feel bad about the wasted effort. The other was a product of a casual suggestion the boss had made to someone on Melissa's team. The offhand comment took on a life of its own as the person thought it was a formal request. Through this conversation, her boss began to understand how she was unintentionally triggering microstress for Melissa and her team. They agreed to a quick check-in strategy to avoid these situations in the future.

On one level, Melissa and her manager learned how to communicate a little better. This improvement translated into concrete changes in both women's actions. Even when the boss couldn't avoid asking the team to do something—she was responding to the CEO's requests, after all—she could take a different tack. She could quickly point Melissa to the right people in the organization to ask for help when she needed to coordinate with other departments so that she didn't waste time trying to get on their overloaded calendars. Occasionally, the boss would step in to help with something herself. She and Melissa became a more coherent team.

When we asked Melissa how she herself created stress, she was a little surprised. In her mind, she didn't create microstress; she helped solve it. She saw herself as a key supporter of everyone in her life. But shifting perspective exposed the truth. With some prodding, she discovered that she did create stress. Melissa would try to respond to her boss's rapidly changing priorities by re-coordinating her team through email. And because she couldn't finish her work until she'd gotten through the family needs that dominated her evenings—homework, sports, school events, dinners—she would start sending emails at 10 p.m. or get up as early as

4 a.m. to catch up. Of course, by then, she was tired and distracted, and half the time her notes were ambiguous. She often got replies asking for clarification. Unintentionally, she was creating stress as people worried about their own full plates. She was also encouraging the always-on climate, which was the last thing she had intended.

To avoid spreading this microstress to her team, Melissa made one simple change. She still wrote the emails after 10 p.m. to match her pattern of work, but she scheduled them to be sent at 8 a.m. the next day. And she instituted standing meetings twice a week to help the team coordinate as a group and to avoid the myriad—and sometimes misaligned—one-off interactions that her emails were driving.

She also found that people—especially her peers and team—were attuned to and reacting to her microstress. She was passing microstress on to them, which made them fret and in turn send more emails and meeting requests to make sure she was good with their work. These requests for reassurance added to the microstress she was emitting. The pattern created a sort of echo chamber of microstress.

She found that scheduling meetings with ten-minute breaks in between helped her (and others) recenter. Entering the next meeting, she was less likely to project her microstress onto her team. Sometimes, she would use part of the break to meditate for five minutes. She started getting more active in group texts with friends, firing off a joke or sharing a story on the ridiculousness of an experience. Here messages immediately got a response. Not only did these brief, lively contacts with friends help center her during the day, but they also helped her renew the connections that she had unintentionally let lapse over the past few years. The humor, she found, was as effective as meditation was in creating separation from the microstress. And the connection and knowing that people were there and cared stayed with her through the day.

Two insights hit Melissa directly when she pondered which microstresses she could rise above. First, she was spending too much time trying to dissect some political maneuverings with her peers. She hadn't been aware of this habit until she went through this exercise. She kept bringing up minor annoyances with her peer group that didn't actually affect her day-to-day work. "I found myself doing silly things like trying to calculate how many vacation days one of my colleagues had taken and whether he was still in compliance, or trying to anticipate which of my peers would be sucking up to our boss," she told us. When we asked her how these annoyances affected her, she recognized that for the most part they didn't. "I realize those are a big waste of my time—and my focus."

The second insight came from the final category we asked Melissa about in the exercise, one she had not considered until we reflected on her responses. She told us about feeling hurt that she was not invited on a ski trip with close friends from college, something she hadn't realized was happening until she saw their happy photos on Facebook. She recognized that she might have let her connections outside of work and her immediate family slide in recent years as work had taken over her life. So, we asked her to focus on what microstress relievers had disappeared from her life. In the past, even when promotions consumed her time and energy, she had still held on to two outside groups that meant a lot to her: a dog agility training group (she raised dogs competitively at a regional level in agility courses) and a local community choral group that met every two months to sing and hang out. She had been active in both groups for more than ten years and had formed powerful friendships. So, it was not only the activities that provided her with some stress relief but also the camaraderie with the people in those groups. With this latest promotion and her two children hitting a stretch during which she needed to be more involved in their activities, she ultimately gave up both groups. Not intentionally, of course. But both groups slid off her calendar to the point that her dog had fallen so far behind on his training that he was no longer compatible with the group, and she couldn't remember the last time she'd sung for pleasure.

With this exercise, she saw how much those two groups had done to counter the microstress in her life. "I didn't realize how these people centered me until I thought about this grid," she told us. "I think those groups helped me keep the work BS in perspective. I used to just laugh at it. But when I reflected on this table, I realized I had gotten more consumed with it at work. And I didn't have any outside connections to counterbalance that. Worse yet, I was spending the scarce time I had with my husband and my children talking about work BS and not more important things."

For Melissa, this simple exercise of examining and categorizing microstresses helped her construct a concrete plan of action. She would schedule emails for the morning, text friends during the day for reprieves, stop worrying about inconsequential slights, and stop micromanaging her children. These constituted a concrete plan—one that she had a realistic chance of completing.

As you work your way through this same exercise, think about small ways you can begin to change the patterns in your life. There are several ways you can do this:

- **Identify opportunities to push back.** In the previous chapters, we suggested practices that can help you lessen the effect of microstresses and prevent them from becoming chronic. In this exercise, the key is to be specific. Identify a few microstresses that are affecting you. Come up with concrete strategies for pushing back on the specific microstressors, as Melissa did. "Stop responding to notifications in real time" is probably not achievable. But "Turn off Slack notifications between 6 p.m. and 8 a.m." is both more concrete and actionable.

- **Change how you interact with the microstress.** Consider whether you are contributing to the problem in some way, perhaps without even knowing it. Even small shifts in dialogue make a difference: "What I thought of as an innocent remark," one midlevel manager told us, "my boss heard as me questioning his ability. I changed the first word of the sentence so instead of making a statement, I was asking a question. And it altered the entire dynamics of relationship." For this manager, "You don't want us to do a quality control round" became "Do you want us to do a quality control round?" Such subtle changes can soften the entire interaction.

- **Look for opportunities to reset relationships.** One executive found herself paired with a difficult colleague during a training session on recognizing implicit bias. Neither thought they had any implicit bias, but the training helped both of them realize that they had subtly staked out what they thought was a moral high ground. This became an opportunity to better understand one another, taking some of the heat out of their interactions when they might disagree. Take the time to understand what might be driving rifts in relationships to overcome them. One strategy is to pivot to what another person is passionate about in their lives—personal or professional. This tack often helps uncover common ground you might not have been aware of.

- **Disconnect from the stress.** For some microstresses, you won't be able to push back or rise above them. So, consider distancing yourself or separating from the source of the stress entirely. That doesn't mean you have to cut people out of your life completely. A distancing strategy can be temporary. You can decline social commitments that pull you into behavior you don't want, or you might recommend different non-stress-triggering ways to get together with those same friends. Meet for dinner before heading to the baseball game rather than spilling out into a local bar afterward, when alcohol-fueled tensions inevitably lead to an argument. When you can't see another path to minimizing or eliminating a microstress that's taking a heavy toll, consider disconnecting.

The happiest people in our interviews were willing to change, or distance themselves from, negative relationships like those with difficult relatives, friends, or colleagues, only seeing them in group settings. One interviewee told us that a woman in her morning walking group dominated conversations, griping about her husband at a level that the interviewee found uncomfortable to listen to. Eventually she started feigning scheduling challenges and instead met a couple of the members for one-on-one walks on weekends. Repeatedly we found that those who were able to disconnect from an unbearable source of microstress were happier. We interviewed people who left jobs, selectively turned down promotions that would come with reporting to a difficult boss, let go of friendships because of excess drama or negativity, and moved away from colleagues whom they loved but who caused them too much work. And they all retrospectively said it was absolutely the right thing to do.

Lesson 1: Move beyond Microstress to Small Moments of Connection

After we finished the exercise of identifying the microstresses she could work on improving, we asked Melissa a different question: What helps you counter the effects of microstress in your life?

For Melissa, this question generated the most unexpected insight from the process. Very little in her life gave her a break from the everyday challenges of her work and home life. She had let connections outside work and her immediate family slide as work had taken over. As described earlier, she had allowed the responsibilities of work and children to preclude activities that had given her emotional balance. She had stopped attending both her dog agility group and the community chorus that she had enjoyed so much.

She had never considered how much she had lost when the demands of work and home had caused her to slowly disconnect from friends and other connections outside work. Although she was unaware of their importance at the time, these outside relationships had provided her with a kind of social resilience to the battering of microstress she faced every day.

As life gets busy, all of us, like Melissa, tend to fall out of groups and passions that once engaged us, and we let work become the sole focus of our lives. We become narrower versions of ourselves, with limited opportunities to realize our full potential both at work and in our personal lives.

One of the most important insights we gained from the happiest people in our research was that other people are not only critical to helping you keep microstress in perspective but essential to helping you build a full, rich life. Few people find happiness in isolation.

Every model of happiness we've found in our research makes clear that personal well-being depends on authentic, personal relationships. One of the longest-running studies of adult life, what's known as the Grant Study, followed Harvard alumni (including John F. Kennedy) for nearly eighty years, collecting data on their physical and mental health.[1] The study's most significant conclusion was that the single biggest determinant of happiness and well-being over a lifetime was not fame or fortune but the quality of personal relationships. "Taking care of your body is important, but tending to your relationships is a form of self-care too," concluded Robert Waldinger, director of the study. "That, I think, is the revelation."[2]

There's an old saying that if you find one true friend in your lifetime, then you have been truly blessed. But our research suggests that a single friend is not enough. You need a variety of relationships (not only close friends) to help you get through the reality of living in a cauldron of microstress. Achieving overall well-being involves developing strategies to combat microstress—and live a fulfilling life—in three key areas: resilience, physical well-being, and purpose. In these areas, your connections with others will play a critical role. The key lies with both the authenticity and the diversity of the relationships. The most significant impact comes from being connected with people who unite around some interest—poetry, religion, singing, tennis, or activism, for example—but who come from different career, socioeconomic, educational, or age groups. The shared interests tend to create authentic and trusted interactions, and the diversity of perspectives helps expand the way we see the world and our place in it. We are shaped by the people and experiences, and our lives become multidimensional. And yet in spite of how important relationships are to our happiness, too many of us let them slip as the years roll by.

People who told us positive life stories invariably described authentic connections with two, three, or four groups outside of work: athletic pursuits, volunteer work, civic or religious communities, book or dinner clubs, and so on. Often, one of the groups supported physical health—through nutrition, mindfulness, and exercise practices. They were often surprising relationships, ones that might seem improbable or a mismatch. But they provided something meaningful.

The ten percenters in our interviews consciously build meaningful connections with other people into their day-to-day lives in ways that help them rise above much of the noise of microstress in their lives and focus on what matters most to them. And to be clear, this group wasn't necessarily extroverts who found time to keep up with a wide range of friends and social connections. The common thread is *dimensionality*—building and maintaining connections with a variety of people, often in small ways. Done right, your relationships with other people can become a kind of force field against the inevitable barrage of microstress. But meaningful relationships require you to take deliberate actions daily. What's more, at critical transition periods in your life, you need to maintain these relationships even more, so you don't default into a defensive posture, become unidimensional, and simply absorb the stress coming at you.

Lesson 2: Beware of Losing Dimensionality

Consider the trajectory of Chris, a tech executive who had been on the career fast track since his early twenties. When he was recruited by a hot Silicon Valley company, he found himself drawn to the lavish off-sites, company perks like box seats at sporting events, and extensive access to cutting-edge technology. Having been identified as a high potential, Chris was part of an exclusive club at work. However, the price of membership was steep. He was expected to be available to his colleagues 24-7, and the travel took him away from home for days at a time. He stopped making personal plans, unsure of what his work would demand at any given time. He found himself eating dinner alone in front of his computer late at night rather than with his wife.

At the same time, work had become deeply competitive. Collaboration with colleagues felt more like a game to see who was on top at any given moment. He was put off by the behavior of his superiors and their sense of entitlement. When one executive regaled young recruits with stories of his personal life that involved keeping his wife and mistress from finding out about each other, Chris paused. He wondered where he was heading.

Chris took some personal time off and talked with his wife about what was most important to him and to them as a couple. They discussed the professional treadmill he was on and decided that though his career should continue to be important to him, they weren't going to measure success the way that many people around them did. They made a conscious choice to "live an ordinary life, extraordinarily well," in his wife's words. "If success looks like the next promotion, or the next new car, or whatever it is, you're always in the race," he told us. "It just moves the goalpost further out for the next time. And so, you'll never get there."

That soul-searching led Chris to define his success through six life roles: a physically healthy person, a spiritual being, an organizational thought leader, a concerned citizen, a family member, and a friend. This clear, perhaps formal blueprint of the person he wanted to be helped him to prioritize his time. These roles, of course, also had to fit in with his wife's goals and vision for their life together, so their conversations had to sync up with her priorities as well. No one thing could dominate.

One night, as Chris sat on a rocking chair on his front porch, he had an epiphany. His different life roles should not be a source of conflict but should create synergy—they should be fused, in his words. "And at that moment," he said, "it never became even a conversation in my life about work-life balance. It was about the entirety of having these things fuse together that made that trade-off go away, and it became a much more innovative way to make decisions and to look at things. The realization for me was that I will only be able to accomplish what I hope to do professionally if my entire life is filled with choices that are meaningful to me. It has to be integrated. And it just sunk in at a deep level. I have to do both."

Chris explained the result: "My definition of success is synthesis- and integration-congruent and a deep realization that I'm only as good in my career as I am in my family and in my friendships and so forth." Wanting to capture his insight, Chris said, he "set out to articulate a personal mission statement and what my obituary will say, and then translate that into six life roles." Therefore, every time he makes a discretionary choice on how to spend his time, it must feed into his desire to fulfill the roles that are important to him.

Chris has done two things that we can all learn from, even if our goals are different. First, he defined the roles that mattered to him. This clarity gives him something specific to measure his time against. And second, he has woven relationships into the habits that sustain these roles. Doing so creates a stickiness that enables him to stay committed and maintain authentic relationships that are a source of joy, purpose, and resilience in his day-to-day life.

For instance, Chris relies on a Sunday soccer game with the neighborhood dads and their kids to help him fulfill his physical health role and his roles as a family member and friend. At these games, he spends quality time with his kids and has lighthearted contact with his neighbors once a week. They tease each other about their slowing speed or jokingly trash-talk one another, but they see each other as genuine friends who support one another. After one father shared that his lawn service had dumped huge piles of mulch on his driveway and blocked the garage, Chris and some of the other dads and kids turned up at his house after the game with shovels in hand. "You guys saved my weekend!" he told them. The group developed an easy cycle of reciprocity, helping one another out from time to time. Seeing how much they helped their neighbor with the mulch helped reinforce how important being a good neighbor was to him. And it helped him demonstrate to his children what he (and, he hoped, they) stood for.

And second, to ensure that he remains committed to other parts of his life, Chris created rituals and routines. Every Sunday, he spends a few minutes reviewing the week, a practice that helps him be accountable for what he considers most important to him. "Did I devote time to my spirituality this week? What did I do to be a concerned citizen this week? Can I prioritize my friends this coming week?" and so on. Chris's six roles are not a secret. He talks about them regularly with his wife, family, and colleagues, and they've all played a role in helping shape and refine them over the years. And that exercise, in turn, has brought him a clear sense of purpose, one he has shaped deliberately with the people who matter most to him. "This is my version of a life well lived," he told us. "I decided early on what mattered most to me, and I've worked hard to stick to that."

Lesson 3: Build and Maintain Your Own Multidimensional Life

Ten percenters like Chris work at building and maintaining dimensionality in their lives, even when it might be challenging to do so because of the demands of work and family. You can do the same thing by adopting some of their best practices:

- **Structure your interactions.** Maintain a diverse network of friends and connections, and structure interactions in a way that helps them stick. You might schedule on your calendar the activities that are core to your involvement with groups you care about and hold those times sacred. It could be twice-a-month dinners, monthly theater outings, weekly tennis or basketball games, daily walks, or annual vacations. The key is to hold the time sacred and commit to being there for each other. Ideally, the interactions accomplish more than one goal, as Chris's activities did. A father-daughter soccer group ticks off time with family and friends. Walking groups combine physical activity with time with friends. Joining a local political group to help write postcards to flood politicians with feedback on a cause fulfills your personal purpose with spending time with a different set of people with whom you share a mutual value. Even a fantasy football league actively connects you to friends outside work while allowing you to blow off steam.

- **Go with the flow.** Chris was rigorous in his structure and planning for multidimensionality. You don't have to be so structured. Some people allow life to unfold a little more fluidly and embrace what emerges. This involves being willing to take advantage of emergent opportunities rather than defaulting to finding excuses for why some activity or event won't work for you. Be open to plan B. For example, rather than plan the exact right group of people to get together for dinner or drinks, something we all know can take months to get right if we don't give up before that in frustration, one person we interviewed broadcasts a dinner invitation to a wide array of friends: "We are going out for drinks or to listen to this music on this day. Would anyone like to come?" This approach worked well. "We never had the same group twice," he told us. "Sometimes I would be surprised by the people who would come, but that always made it interesting and helped me develop some new friendships."

- **Lean into the moment.** Find ways to appreciate the micromoments as they come up. Make deliberate choices to be with people and stay fully present with them when you're together, even if time is limited. One leader described how much he treasures the half-hour ride to horseback riding lessons with his daughter, talking about what was going on in her world. That is the only time in a week that he can count on having one-on-one time with her, and he made the most of it staying totally focused on her during the entire commute. Another easy win is to not rush off after an activity— walking, yoga, church, or a local musical event. Lingering and making conversation is a great way to connect informally with others who might have a different perspective on life.

- **Broaden your perspective of life.** While many of us seek emotional support from those closest to us, this practice can have an unintended consequence of reinforcing our feelings in a way that fosters self-pity or anger rather than resilience. Connect with people outside your closest circle of family and friends to overcome this. One highly successful consulting executive cherishes a weekly Bible study with men from his church. In hearing about the challenges of community members who needed and received aid from his study group, he developed greater empathy for others' struggles and a greater appreciation of the positive aspects of his life. The interactions not only help him keep his own travails in perspective but inspire him to proactively help others with less means. The sessions became a major source of purpose and perspective in his life.

Notably, these recommendations aren't purely about establishing work-life balance, though for some of our interviewees, that was one of the benefits. Rather, having a multidimensional life—deeply embedded in authentic connection with others—is fundamental to your well-being. Connections with others, formal and informal, helps you thrive both in and out of work. "Engaging with other people . . . trains your brain (like training a coordinated group of muscles) to develop brain circuits for managing your own reactions, responses, and emotions," said neurologist Joel Salinas. There's also a healthy distraction component because emotional burdens don't weigh on you as much when you're immersed in a multidimensional life. "You tend not to ruminate on your problems when you are around other people that engage your full attention in a positive way," Salinas said.

There's ample evidence that this kind of presence with other people helps generate more creative problem-solving and reduces the physical effects of stress, such as high blood pressure. And as our ten percenters found, engaging with other people helps give you a better sense of how to frame an issue, especially if you can zoom out to see it more clearly in context. You're more likely to be able to think, "I'm not the only person who has had this experience." Or, "Other people have it much worse than I do." That kind of engagement with others can help right-size microstress.

Finally, Salinas says, having multiple dimensions in life means that your identity is not anchored on only one activity—such as work. Research suggests that high achievers in their twenties and early thirties are often vulnerable to burnout, Salinas says, because they haven't developed other dimensions. "Their identity becomes more and more anchored on work. That means the positive things at work can bring extreme highs,

COACHING BREAK

Examining the Multidimensional Nature of Your Network

Use table 5-2 to see whether you connect with others on at least two or three dimensions outside of work. In the first column, list the various spheres of interaction. In the second column, identify whether and how you connect with others in each of the four spheres. In the third column, identify ways you can engage in activities and groups in each sphere and add opportunities for personal growth into your life. In the last column, note any concrete actions you can take to truly immerse yourself in these groups or activities. (In table 5-2, this last column has been filled in with examples of actions one interviewee planned to take.) As you do so, consider two strategies that our interviewees often found successful:

- Reach back to *activities* from your past. Many interviewees had dropped out of pursuits they had enjoyed in their younger days, but the foundations remained for them to easily reengage in those activities—such as a community basketball team, the local church choir, or fishing on weekends—and to use them to launch into a new group of friends.

- Reach back to *relationships* from your past. The ten percenters often renewed relationships that had been neglected over time and maintained them with structured activities, such as monthly dinners at people's homes, an ongoing virtual Monopoly game, or annual outings with college friends through chat and Zoom calls between get-togethers.

TABLE 5-2

Assessing, and improving on, the dimensions of your network

Spheres	How do you connect with others along this dimension?	What steps can you take to build connection in this sphere? – Consider *activities* and *relationships* you can reach out to from your past. – Identify groups you can join, people you can reach out to, or ways that you can reallocate your time to make these connections a priority.	Example actions
Friends/community: Often forged through collective activity such as athletic endeavors or book or dinner clubs.			Join the basketball team at the local community center.
Civic/volunteer: Contributing to meaningful groups that create purpose and bring us in contact with diverse but like-minded people.			Volunteer your skills and experience to teach financial literacy to kids who need the extra help.
Family: Through actions like caring for family, modeling valued behaviors and living traditions and values with extended family.			Prioritize family traditions such as dinnertime together and cooking recipes handed down through the generations.
Spiritual/artistic: Interactions around religion, music, art, poetry, and other aesthetic spheres of life that put work in a broader context.			Rekindle your passion for classical music by dusting off your violin and joining a local chamber music group.

but the negative things can bring extreme lows too." The mere act of connecting with others, having informal conversations, sharing mutual interests, or just briefly seeing the world from another perspective is a powerful antidote to the daily toll of microstress. But as we go through life, we are pulled in so many directions that we tend to let go of the activities and relationships we once enjoyed, because we're too busy.

The percentage of people who say they don't have a single close friend has quadrupled in the past thirty years, according to the Survey on American Life.[3] Nearly half of those surveyed say they've lost touch with friends over the past year, while one in ten reported having lost touch with *most* of their friends. This development is not healthy. Salinas's research demonstrates that even simply having someone you can count on to listen to you is associated with greater cognitive resilience—a measure of your brain's ability to function better than would be expected for the amount of physical aging or disease-related changes in the brain. "Being connected with other people seems to provide a buffer to the negative effects of brain aging and disease," he said. "Enough that your cognitive age might be closer to that of someone who is four years younger. It's quite literally good for your health."[4]

To enjoy overall well-being, you must develop strategies not only to combat stress but also to help you live the life you want to live with resilience, physical health, and purpose. For each of these three pillars, your connections with others will play a critical role. Surviving the onslaught of microstress doesn't have to be a solitary pursuit. In fact, it shouldn't be. The next chapters will show that the authenticity and diversity of relationships in your life are not just perks of a satisfying life. They are integral to it.

Chapter 6

Where to Find Resilience

 KEY INSIGHTS

- **Resilience is associated with better performance at work, the ability to avoid burnout, and can even fend off physical or mental illnesses.**

- We tend to think of resilience as something we're born with or that we have to dig deep to find within ourselves. But it also comes from specific kinds of support you can draw from your network during difficult times. You are more likely to weather professional and personal setbacks more smoothly **if you have built a diverse set of connections and know how to draw support from them.**

- **Those interactions can help us find resilience in moments of microstress in several ways:**

  - Providing empathic support so that we can release our emotions and stay balanced
  - Helping us see and pursue a path forward
  - Providing perspective when setbacks happen
  - Helping us manage surges at work or at home
  - Making sense of people or politics

      ◦ Encouraging us to laugh at ourselves and the situation

      ◦ Enabling us to unplug and take a break from challenges

- People who are more resilient are adept at knowing **what form of resilience support they need to move through tough stretches.** You need various types of support, not just deep friendships or your family's empathy, to get through the daily microstress gauntlet.

- You have to **develop your resilience network—and maintain it—** not only to survive everyday microstresses but also to ensure it's there when you need it for major setbacks.

An anesthesiologist we'll call Michael was used to navigating the slog of everyday challenges he faced as head of his department at a highly respected hospital. Because he was responsible for several hundred doctors and nurses, his days were pulsing with microstresses: administrative priorities shuffled and reshuffled, misalignments of goals with other department heads, bureaucratic requirements draining his capacity to get work done, demands from big donors causing him to lose focus on his own priorities, and so on. But he could weather all these storms because he had built up an array of connections both in and out of the hospital, and these relationships helped him manage the microstress. And so on most days, he thrived while juggling the demands of his high-pressure work life. But all that changed during the pandemic.

Because anesthesiology is not a specialty that could resort to remote telemedicine, Michael and his team had to turn up for work in an overwhelmed hospital day after day. The burden of being responsible for both a team he cared deeply about and the lives of a huge volume of patients affected by the pandemic was crushing. "For two months, I wasn't sleeping at night," he told us. "I was sending my team into battle with inadequate protection and not even really knowing how many of them would get sick." Routinely putting in sixteen-hour days, Michael was having to determine how and when his team would work in these extraordinary circumstances. "There were nights and weekends when some [colleagues] called me crying on the phone," he recounted. "Let's face it, they were scared for their lives."

But Michael was well prepared for such an intense period of stress. He had spent years building authentic connections with a variety of people who had helped him navigate the everyday microstresses of his work. So even when the stress was ramped up beyond what he had experienced before, he had a set of go-to people who could help take it down by removing some of the microstresses that were triggered when he and his team had to change the way they worked through the pandemic. Michael's network offered support ranging from taking over tasks that would free up his time to lending his department extra resources to simply helping him think through how he could tackle each day's challenges. "I can't tell you how grateful I am for my colleagues," he told us. "I'm not sure I even thought about how much we help each other in everyday life until then."

Michael's previous efforts to build a network of personal and professional connections paid off when he needed resilience to navigate the daily microstresses that accumulated at breathtaking speed and volume during the pandemic. If he hadn't already developed relationships with an array of people in his hospital, he would have suffered through the setbacks of the pandemic much more deeply.

For most of us, the challenges we experienced during the pandemic were a test of our resilience. We may not have been afraid for our lives on a daily basis the way Michael was, but our lives were suddenly filled with microstresses that we had never faced before. The pandemic was an important reminder of how our connections with others, both personal and professional, can be integral to surviving periods of extraordinary stress. Building your connections and tapping them in everyday life can help you become more agile for setbacks of any scale.

When resilience is baked into our everyday lives, it plays a critical role in our professional success and our physical and mental health. There's ample research to suggest that resilient people are more successful pro-fessionally and have an edge when competing for jobs or promotions.[1] Resilient people are better able to cope with demanding jobs and eco-nomic hardship.[2] Studies have also shown that resilience protects people from burnout and is associated with higher levels of hope and optimism.[3] And resilient people are also less likely to become physically or mentally ill during challenging times and tend to have higher levels of work sat-isfaction.[4] When the environment around them changes and their skills become outdated, people with resilience are better able to learn new ones.[5] We all need resilience to keep the daily battering of microstresses from derailing us.

The ten percenters in our research have shown that resilience can be nurtured and built not from digging deep to find some kind of inner grit but through our interactions with other people. And as mentioned ear-lier, resilience doesn't depend on ride-or-die friends who have your back at all times. You can build resilience in small moments of authentic con-nection with a range of people in your life.

It requires a kind of agility to reach out to the right people in your network in small but powerful ways for the right kind of support at the right time. For example, sometimes we need empathy, but then too much of it can lead us to wallow in self-pity and not take steps forward. At other times, we might need advice on a path forward, a new perspective, or just the ability to laugh at the absurdity of life. Small moments can reset us and keep us from spiraling into negativity. In this chapter, we'll explain how this works—and how you can ensure that you're building and maintaining a robust resilience network that can help you survive both the daily onslaught of microstress and the periods of significant setbacks in your life.

What a Resilience Network Looks Like

Most of us count on close family and friends to support us during chal-lenging times. But people *outside our inner circle* can also play a valuable role in helping us be resilient to the routine microstress we face. The ten percenters were particularly adept at building and nurturing their networks in ways that helped them navigate daily microstresses. And then when they were dealt more challenging setbacks, that preexisting network became critical to their resilience.

Resilience is found not just in having people to lean on when times get tough, but in the *interactions themselves*—the conversations that validate our plans, reframe our perspective, help us laugh and feel authentic with others, or just encourage us to get back up and try again. Resilience is essential to coping with microstress. Bouncing back from any individual microstress helps avoid a pileup of microstresses that drag you down. Here's how you can find resilience in moments of microstress through reaching out to connections in your life.

Seek Empathic Support So You Can Release Your Emotions and Stay Balanced

Sometimes when you're going through challenges, you're not necessarily interested in advice or guidance from others. Sometimes you just want someone who will help you feel heard and validated. This kind of support helps you keep your emotional balance. Many spouses have learned this lesson the hard way after offering practical solutions in response to their partner's complaints, not realizing their spouse wasn't looking for advice. When these conversations go right, people get what they need at the moment. "I'm free to vent and talk and feel what I feel," one successful banker shared with us. "And then my husband will say, 'Don't worry, it'll be OK.' Of course, I know that's not always true, but when he says that, it soothes me."

Empathic support offsets microstress in three ways. It allows for emotional release. Getting angry in a safe space allows you to move to more-rational responses. It also provides validation. Someone else confirms that what you're dealing with is hard or that your frustration makes sense. Validation cuts off the microstress of self-doubt or feelings of being in the wrong. And finally, empathic support demonstrates caring. Just knowing that someone is there for you can have a calming effect and give you the confidence that comes with not having to face adversity alone. One interviewee described the feeling he got from others in his church group when he'd been through a particularly hectic time at work: "It's the power of presence. Folks didn't even have to say anything. They would just sit and spend time with me, and that alone let me know that they cared about me."

Empathic support with microstress isn't exclusively about soothing yourself. You can use it as temporary support that will help steel your resolve to move through a difficult situation. For example, Gabe, a technology executive, relies heavily on his wife and a core group of friends for empathic support. His wife works at the same company, and they have what he calls "mutual bitch sessions" about work. Just saying things out loud seems to bring Gabe greater clarity and calm. His wife often reassures him that the issues he faces would be tough for anyone to handle and reminds him that he can be his own worst critic. Gabe also lets off steam with his diverse group of friends who range from IT people like himself to a professional cartoonist. When he's with them, he feels he can joke around and be himself. "Just being able to commiserate with them recharges my batteries," he explained. "There's comfort in knowing you're not alone in muddling through." Even that little bit of perspective helps Gabe regroup and find a path through his challenge.

Ten Percenter Tips

- **Seek out people who have common experiences or challenges.** It's wonderful when a loved one has your back in a difficult time, but they don't always fully understand what you're going through. Look for people who have walked in your shoes before. You might touch base with the person who held your job before you and ask how they navigated your manager's mercurial temper. Finding someone who can listen and offer perspective because they've been in a similar situation is a powerful source of resilience.

- **Build traditions, not obligations.** Maintain connections by creating structured times when you're committed to getting together with people in your network. Often, these can become traditions and inviolable spaces for social connection. One senior leader at a consulting firm told us that she had maintained an annual girls' weekend with her best friends from college for decades. "Just one weekend a year, but we all commit to it, no matter what else is going on in our lives." They managed this longtime contact through new babies, moves to other countries, and even personal health struggles. Because they're not in each other's daily lives, they feel free to share their struggles with one another without judgment. And this camaraderie carries over into a group chat that is an almost-daily source of support for them throughout the year.

- **Pay it forward.** Provide empathic support to others. Too often we can default to being the person who tries to solve someone else's problem, but there's enormous value in simply being a good listener. Consider something as simple as starting with "That sounds really hard" and "I can imagine how difficult this is for you," rather than defaulting to giving advice. Talk less, listen more.

Find People Who Help You See and Pursue a Path Forward

Venting may feel good, but eventually you need a practical way to move forward. Relationships help in two ways. They give you actual models for moving forward—you can ask someone who has faced such a situation how they handled it. And good relationships motivate you to move forward; the other person motivates and may even hold you accountable for actually doing something rather than just wallowing in self-pity.

People who are more resilient take advantage of others' ideas more expansively to envision alternative routes forward. And by doing this rapidly in small moments, they keep microstresses from magnifying. Improve your resilience by building ties with people who can help you break down problems into smaller and more manageable chunks, find new ways to make progress on challenging tasks, and motivate you to act.

COACHING BREAK

Assessing the Strength of Your Resilience Network

Most of us can point to a few people who helped us get through really challenging times, but how strong is your day-to-day resilience network? Next to each of the following questions in table 6-1, write down the names of a person (or people) who provide this support in your daily life. In the final column, add a brief description of how they help you.

Review your checklist; this is your current resilience network. Is it robust? Are there a variety of names on your list? Are there some blanks? You might also check to see if there is one person—maybe your spouse—who is listed over and over. Overreliance on a single person means your

TABLE 6-1

My sources of resilience

Source of resilience	Name(s)	How they helped you
Who provides **empathic support** so that you can release your emotions and stay balanced? This person lets you vent, is able to commiserate, or just makes you feel like there is another person there to listen.		
Who helps you see a **path forward**? When you need practical advice, this person helps you with suggestions, explains how they handled something similar, or lets you see some of the options you could consider.		

resilience network might not be that resilient! If you haven't built a solid network before you encounter challenging times, you're far more likely to be derailed by a setback.

Who gives you a different **perspective**? When you are overthinking or about to drown in self-pity, this person helps you to see that it's not as bad as you think.		
Who helps you **manage a surge** at work or at home? When you are overwhelmed by demands, this person may come through with resources or their own time and talents to help you through.		
Who helps you to **make sense** of people or politics? This person might have more experience or a broader view and can help you to better understand others' behavior.		
Who helps you **laugh** at yourself or your situation? This person may diffuse the tension by injecting humor.		
Who helps you **unplug or take a break** from your challenges? You join this person in doing something—a sport, some hiking, a getaway—that is completely unrelated to your challenge, so your mind and body get a break.		

Empathy can come from anyone who cares about you. A smaller subset of people in your network can help you see and pursue a path forward. Look for people who can speak to the specifics of a situation. They may know how the company runs, or they may have had interactions with the particular person who is causing your microstress so that their advice is specific and actionable. Seek people who can help you figure out what to do! The same person can fill multiple roles in your life—an empathic listener can also help you plan a path forward. But you need to make sure you have a variety of people in your network so that you don't rely too heavily on any one person to play multiple roles.

Consider Isabel, the leader of a manufacturing unit, who had both work colleagues and family to turn to when microstresses piled up on her. For some situations, she found help through her siblings, both of whom worked in similar jobs in different organizations. She might call her sister and say, "Hey, I'm really stalled getting people to buy in to a new system. What strategies have you used to engage people to want to be part of the change?" When Isabel went from overseeing a small group to leading a much bigger and broader one, she leaned on her brother's experience in delegating.

Ten Percenter Tips

- **Develop "fish or cut bait" counselors.** These connections are good at helping you see which path to choose and which to leave behind. You lean on them precisely because you know they'll give pointed advice. Their role is more than just being a sounding board. These are people you count on to help you make the right call. The person might be a trusted professional mentor, a close work colleague who knows you and the situation well, or even your parent who has been through similar challenges in life. Note which people in your network are good at helping you cut to the chase to make decisions—people who say things like "Don't waste your time on that" or "If I were you, I'd just go in and ask for the promotion"—and lean on them for that purpose.

- **Find your truth tellers.** A truth teller is someone you trust to be straight with you—and someone you won't dismiss when they say things that are hard for you to hear. They are vital for resetting your perspective and getting you to see the bigger picture when it's hard to. When she was devastated that she didn't get a promotion, one interviewee started to wallow in self-pity. But after a day or two of empathy, her husband became a truth teller. "In the grand scheme of things, you really have nothing to complain about," he told her. "You have a good job and a great family. Get over it." It doesn't have to be a person you're this close to, either. The ten percenters in our research often spoke about a boss they had early in their career or the first person who hired them. They reflected on how important those relationships continued to be because they respected what the person had to say, even when the truth was difficult to hear. As one senior manager explained, "We had so much trust between us, whether it was something about work or I just needed perspective on 'How do I do this? Have you been through this before?'"

Seek Perspective When Setbacks Happen

It can be easy to spiral into a panic when you're faced with obstacles, but seeing events in a broader perspective can put them in a different, more positive light. This widening of our perspective is sometimes referred to as *de-catastrophizing*. But it can require heavy cognitive lifting to do this on our own. We tend to fare much better when we have others to help us step back, reframe, and see our problems in a broader context.

For example, when Charlie discovered that he had been cut out of an important meeting, he wanted to go raging into the director's office. But recognizing his own rising anger, he instead called a trusted colleague who was not part of his group. Given that she didn't have the same wounded feelings that Charlie did, she coolly helped reset his perspective. "Don't do anything today," she advised. "Your manager is juggling a lot of balls right now. There may be a good reason you weren't included, or it may have been an oversight. Don't go storming into his office until you know more about what's going on." That was exactly the right advice. A later conversation with the boss confirmed that he was trying to do Charlie a favor by not wasting his time on that meeting. Things are often not as bad as we fear—especially when we see the merit of overcoming challenges as part of reaching larger goals.

Ten Percenter Tips

- **See the world through new lenses.** Try leaning on a trusted mentor or a friend with little to no connection to your work. Fresh perspective from these outsiders helps ameliorate daily microstresses by reminding you of the bigger picture from a less emotional perspective. One particularly effective form of perspective we get from others is the "Knock it off!" variety—someone's blunt advice when you're caught in a rut of overthinking, stressing, or being self-critical. An otherwise supportive spouse or close friend might cut short your descent into self-doubt, saying, "You're spending too much time thinking. Get out of your head."

- **Reinforce your core values.** When microstresses are battering you, build ties with people who help you remember your core values. This person could be a friend who has known you forever, who is decidedly unimpressed with your professional credentials, but who cares about you as a person. Book clubs, prayer groups, or volunteer communities are just a few of the kinds of groups that provided enormous benefit to the ten percenters by providing connection to people who share values but who come from many different walks of life. One ten percenter described talking through difficult career decisions with a childhood friend while they shot hoops together. While playing, his friend called him out. The interviewee recalled, "He was like, 'Dude, since when do you care so much about a fancy title?' and I remembered that he was right. The work I do is more important than the title I have."

Ask for Help to Manage Surges at Work or at Home

Think back to a time when you experienced a sudden surge at work—a late-breaking request from a key client, a difficult period because your team was short-staffed, a high-pressure board presentation. How did you get through that rough patch? If you're like many people, you probably resorted to heroic measures to get it done. You put in extra hours, allowed your concentration to toggle between work and home even when you were trying to be fully present with your family, or perhaps even canceled personal plans. But these extraordinary efforts come at a cost—working harder to survive surges in work (or at home) can throw everything off balance, undermining your sense of control over your life.

A more resilient approach is to ask for help from your network. Take Michael, the anesthesiologist we discussed earlier. Despite the demands of the moment, he wasn't a solitary hero. He drew on the strong working relationship he had with another department head to jointly manage workload surges. Another colleague "lent" him the time of administrative personnel who could help Michael's department stay on top of scheduling and other operational tasks. "At a couple of really important junctures, this helped us from getting overrun," he recalled. What Michael did particularly well during this rough time was to ask for help in small but concrete ways. He told us that just knowing that he had reliable people stepping up to help "allowed me to focus on the most important things during that time."

Ten Percenter Tips

- **Proactively help people in your network.** Don't wait for a crisis to ask people for help or to step in to help others, either. By finding ways to help people even when there's no pressing issue, you establish a basis for future reciprocity. The support you offer can be as simple as making a point to talk up other people and giving credit where credit is due in public settings. Small actions build trust and reciprocity and seed a relationship you can count on for support when surges happen.

- **Make sure your colleagues see you as someone worth helping.** You might go a step or two beyond offering routine help to others when it's not necessarily your responsibility, offering your time or helping others problem-solve when they're in need. Being *that* colleague encourages others to help you when you need it, because they know their assistance will pay off for them in the future.

- **Identify people with shared goals.** Make an effort to build relationships with people who will be eager to help you because their goals and interests intersect with yours. Look for shared goals beyond the obvious; they might not even be part of work. You might coordinate sports team carpooling for your kids, for example.

Find People Who Help You Laugh at Yourself—or the Situation

You know this intuitively: laughter is rejuvenating. But its physiological effects are less well known: laughter activates neural pathways of emotions like joy and mirth, upping serotonin levels and limiting stress hormones like cortisol. It's literally an antidepressant but without the side effects.[6] And there's evidence that we laugh best when we laugh with others. According to linguist Don Nilsen, chuckles and belly laughs seldom happen when we are alone.[7]

This information translates directly into how you can protect yourself against the sting of microstresses. Laughter can help everyone relax and reset to where they can think better, be more creative, and just feel human. As one senior leader expressed, "It kind of lowers the blood pressure, right? It's like, 'Hey, this doesn't have to just be stress and business. We can have fun while we do this.'"

This doesn't mean you have to brush up on your dad jokes to be the funny one in meetings. There are other simple ways to share humor as an antidote for daily microstresses. One HR executive described how his ragtag group of buddies text each other periodically. He'll be in a serious meeting, and one of the guys will send him a text that just cracks him up. It's lighthearted banter, but it helps him to handle the absurd moments of his job. Another leader described a friend whom she can call when she feels like the world is against her. After a while, the friend will say, "OK, enough of that" and launch into a humorous tirade. "It can be so off the wall," said the leader, "but it just stops the train from continuing in the direction of pity."

Ten Percenter Tips

- **Share humor virtually.** Small moments matter when it comes to laughter. The ability to maintain virtual ties with friends who share your sense of humor and who can lighten your mood throughout the day or week is a genuine benefit to the always-on culture. "Sometimes I'm steaming around the house racing to get ready, and that text from one of my friends comes in, and I will stop just long enough to watch a thirty-second TikTok video," one executive told us. "And I'll be in tears laughing before it's done. Some days, that's just enough to prevent me from wallowing in whatever microstresses I'm facing that day." Others told us about forming family chat groups in which they would share family jokes. "When I proudly showed my teenage daughters the 'views' on one of my LinkedIn posts, one of them replied 'Dad, you're totally an influencer now . . .' and I laughed at myself as much as she did."

- **Make light of hard situations.** The ten percenters repeatedly found ways to create humor at the expense of a set of circumstances or even unreasonable stakeholders. One interviewee told us about a meeting in which his manager berated the team for missing a deadline, even though they had been working nights and weekends trying to keep up. It was a no-win moment. As soon as the manager left the room, he turned to his crestfallen teammates and said, "Well, that went well!" The room burst into laughter, diffusing the tension.

- **Use self-deprecating humor.** Self-deprecation removes status from a situation and lets people see your authentic, vulnerable self. The disarming nature of this form of humor can create bonding among team members. One leader described the friction she had with a colleague in another unit. In heated moments, her colleague often had a masterful ability to disarm people by saying something like, "Well, I explained that well!" And they both would laugh. Interjecting humor kept the conflict they had over ideas or methods from becoming too personal and helped them recognize that if the discussion got heated, it was because they both cared.

Make Sense of People or Politics

Microstress is created and re-created when we agonize over a passing comment, worry that we said the wrong thing to the wrong person at the wrong time, or review our emails to make sure we didn't unintentionally offend someone. Feeling like we don't quite get the underlying politics of a situation can throw us off our game and keep us up at night playing and replaying events in our mind. By ourselves, we're unlikely to be able to break through the limits of our own understanding of the political dynamics in a given situation. When we have a trusted ally who sees the political landscape better than we do, we're better able to position our own work and efforts with confidence, rather than worrying unnecessarily about things that don't matter. We spend less time being counterproductive and concerned about the motivations and underlying priorities of other people. And we can feel more self-assured about our own position.

We don't need to have relationships with people who can each help us solve any political problem. But we will benefit from constructing a patchwork of people who play different roles in helping us make sense of politics. For example, maybe we don't realize a particular colleague is under duress to produce results, is worried about their job, or has been burned in the past. Having a well-established colleague help decode what's really gone on can be enormously helpful to reducing our stress.

Enrico, for example, a senior manager in the health-care industry, turned to a group of peers from a prior job when he was feeling uncertain about a conversation with his new boss. When they were discussing some highly confidential material, the boss made a comment about them discussing it so "casually." Enrico kept ruminating over what she meant by that. Did she not trust him?

Fortunately, his former colleagues helped reset Enrico's perspective on what his boss may have meant. Perhaps she was a little nervous herself about having access to the information and that was her way of getting it off her chest. But she clearly trusted Enrico in that conversation. If he hadn't had the opportunity to make sense of it, he told us, "it would have been another dumb thing that I think about at one o'clock in the morning."

Ten Percenter Tips

- **Connect with connectors.** In every organization, there are natural connectors who seem to know people in other offices and departments and who may even be well connected to alumni of the organization. They are a great support for making sense of politics. One high performer told us that one of the most valuable conversations he had every day was the informal chat with someone in IT on the morning shuttle from the parking lot to the office. "I just got a completely different sense of the pulse of the place than I would sitting in my own office all day," he said. Make sure you are part of the connectors' informal network, too. For example, one ten percenter maintained a long-standing relationship with a person in HR, even though they didn't work together. Whenever she was uncertain about proposing a new initiative, the HR person would give her a road map: "Start with this person, then that person, and then you'll have enough support to take it to this committee." The inside information was an invaluable perspective. In turn, when the HR department proposed a new initiative, she was publicly supportive. "We just built a relationship of respect," she told us.

- **Maintain a network of go-to colleagues.** These don't have to be your closest allies in the company. Find people who will share their experience and perspective with you. One rising star in a publishing company said she regularly turned to a colleague with two decades at the company and who was close to retirement. "She and I weren't particularly close, but she was above the political fray. She had amazing instincts and experience, and she was generous in sharing her thoughts on how to handle deadlines and how certain people reacted to being kept out of the loop and so forth."

Find People Who Help You Unplug and Take a Break from Microstress

Breaks are essential to our best work. Research finds that when we come back from a break, our sense of well-being has improved because the break lowered our stress, decreased our emotional exhaustion, and improved our energy levels, leaving us better able to focus.[8] But many people assume that a break means getting away from it all. Most ten percenters, though, say that the breaks they and others take together, even during immersive activities, provided stronger benefits. If we're engaged with other people, it's easier to stop ruminating on personal or professional microstresses.

Bryant, a financial executive, unplugs by spending time with his family, his church, and his motorcycle club. When he's at his job, the work gets all his attention, and when he's with family, it's all about them. Biking is the one thing he can do to get away from both, the primary sources of microstress in his life. As a result, he can completely unwind with the biker club. "It's just a bunch of guys going seventy or eighty miles per hour, out there to do one thing and one thing only, and that's ride and enjoy," he said. "It's the best stress reliever in the world."

Ten Percenter Tips

- **Build networks around shared recreational activities.** Having a recreational network allows you to immerse yourself with other people around an activity you love and to recharge through that activity. One consultant went on a meditation retreat once a year. The group is silent for part of the day and is then allowed to connect and share with other participants at other times. "I found this group to be essential for my overall well-being," he told us. "We can be ourselves, fully, in this group I've come to know very well. I look forward to this retreat every year."

- **Pursue self-improvement with others.** One scientist told us that on every New Year's Day, she made a list of all the books she planned to read. But she seldom made a dent in it until, at her workplace, she joined a book group that met over lunch once a month. Not only was she motivated to keep up with the reading, but she also began to connect with people in other parts of her organization—people she otherwise wouldn't have met.

- **Invest in extended networks.** Ten percenters place a high premium on staying connected to social networks that involve people *who aren't integral to their professional or personal lives*. Carol joined a local outdoor coffee group that was formed in her town during the pandemic. Someone put a notice on a local park's bulletin board, and people just started turning up. They'd meet in that park, sitting spaced out from one another, for a casual conversation once a week. "At first all we talked about was the pandemic," she told us. "But over time, it became a really great way for me to get fresh perspective on life." A media executive joined a local singing group in which she knew nobody. But she loved showing up each week, becoming part of a community she hadn't even know existed. Even though she was an introvert, it was easy to chat and laugh between songs.

Strengthening Your Resilience through Relationships

Are your relationships broad and deep enough to help support you when you hit setbacks? Take these two steps to find out.

1. Identify the Top Sources of Resilience You Need

As described in this chapter, there are seven relational sources of resilience. These sources are not universally or equally important to everyone. Some people might value laughter, while others prefer empathy. Our needs for resilience are personal and shaped by our unique history, personality, and professional and personal circumstances. But collectively, the relationships we develop are a toolbox we can turn to in difficult times and rely on to help us navigate day-to-day challenges.

Using table 6-2, identify the top three sources of resilience out of the seven that you would most like to strengthen in your life. Place a checkmark by those that you would most like to develop.

2. Plan How to Strengthen Your Network

Reflect on the top three sources of resilience you indicated. Connections that yield resilience can be intentionally cultivated in two ways. You can deepen existing relationships or initiate new ones. Use both techniques, but remember that broadening your network helps you develop dimensionality—a rich variety of relationships and connections. Greater dimensionality provides a better perspective on your struggles, offers you a stronger sense of purpose, or simply lets you unplug from your day-to-day struggles. Also remember to cultivate existing and new relationships both in your typical realms of work, family, and friends and beyond those realms.

Write down the names of the people or groups that you want to invest in further. If you want to deepen your relationship with them, place them in the third column. If they are relationships you want to create, place them in the last column. Table 6-2 shows how your chart might look.

TABLE 6-2

My relational sources of resilience

What the connection does	Step 1: Check the sources of relational resilience you'd like to strengthen	Step 2: Strengthen your network	
		Identify strategies to deepen existing relationships	Identify strategies to initiate relationships with new people or groups
Provides empathic support			
Gives you perspective when setbacks happen	X		Make a point of walking to the train at end of the workday with a colleague in another department.
Helps you see a path forward	X	Connect with three peers in adjacent departments for informal sounding board on resolving technical problem.	
Helps you manage surges at work or at home			
Helps you make sense of politics			
Helps you find humor in tough situations			
Enables you to unplug and reset	X	Initiate a monthly book club — send invites to twenty people who I have not seen in a while, and see who shows up.	

The Best Defense Is Preparation

A resilient network won't materialize overnight. As we have shown, ten percenters cultivate and maintain authentic connections from many parts of their life—not only through work but also through athletic pursuits, volunteer work, civic or religious communities, clubs, parents they've met through their children, and so on. Interactions in these spheres provide critical dimensionality, broadening people's identity and opening the aperture on how they look at their lives. We become more (or less) resilient through our interactions with others.

Just as you might be unaware of the dozens of microstresses bombarding you at any given time, you might also not recognize how important an antidote your relationships can be to them. It's in the interactions themselves—conversations that validate our plans, reframe our perspective on a situation, help us laugh and feel authentic, or just encourage us to get back up and try again—that we become resilient. Being connected with others is not just a nice-to-have in our lives; it's essential for our overall well-being. In the next chapter, we'll explore how these same connections can play a critical role in helping us maintain our physical health.

Chapter 7

How to Stay Healthy

 KEY INSIGHTS

- **By our mid-thirties, many of us start to fall out of the activities that once kept us vibrant and physically fit;** we just get too busy to keep up. And we suffer the consequences as our physical health deteriorates.

- **People who avoid this fate don't necessarily have more will-power, more free hours in the day, or better focus** than the rest of us do. Their trajectory to improving their physical health follows a typical pattern in which the activity and their network are intimately interwoven:

  1. Elevate your physical health as a priority.
  2. Share your commitment, to make it visible to others.
  3. Create stickiness through relationships at work and at home.
  4. Reinforce and broaden your identity through activities and connections with others that focus on your well-being.

- **Ten percenters weave their physical health into the relationships around them.** We care about sticking with the activities that make us healthier because we feel connected with the people with whom we share those activities. This connection in turn makes us persist in our pursuit of health, something that other shorter-term solutions—weight-reduction groups, for example—don't do. Intertwining health initiatives and relationships creates a positive pull and desire to be healthy; these efforts go beyond social pressure to remove something negative like excess alcohol consumption or weight gain. Instead they are connected to positive associations with others, making it easier to stick with.

R ebecca, a leader at a major research institution, recounted to us a time when her physical health hit a low point seven years earlier. She had been finishing her part-time MBA and working a full-time job with an hour-long commute. In this timeframe, she had sunk into increasingly bad health habits. On her long commute home, she'd check in with her husband about dinner. Trying to make it easy for her, he'd say, "Just pick up Burger King." Her capacity drained by dozens of microstresses throughout the day, Rebecca couldn't find the emotional bandwidth to object. No way could she whip up a healthy meal when she got home and her husband never volunteered. And so, they ate fast food. A lot. Picking what type of fast food they'd eat became a highlight of her day.

Even worse, exercise was a distant memory for the once-active Rebecca. She was aware that she had fallen into destructive habits, but she couldn't see a way around it. Her life was filled with microstresses—and the secondary consequences of them—that kept pushing her offtrack. For example, neither her husband nor their friends were particularly interested in exercise and nutrition. They found joy in good food and drink, and their social lives revolved around that. Weekends were often consumed with elaborate tailgating parties supporting their favorite football team. Or they regularly met at a local pub for a drink before a late-night restaurant meal. For Rebecca to feel part of the group, she felt she had to go.

She liked them as individuals, but as a group, they tended to fuel each other's worst habits. What she didn't recognize at the time was that each of these invitations was a microstress, subtly challenging her emotional reserves and her identity. Rebecca went with the flow because it was her only social outlet, but she found herself getting more and more miserable in the process.

You would not recognize the former Rebecca if you met her today. When we interviewed her, she was vibrant and healthy. She told us that at some point, she simply decided that she was not the person she wanted to be. "I just felt like the people I was hanging out with weren't the best for me," she recalled. She finally understood that she had built her life around connections with people who didn't value the same things she once did. This group included her husband.

No magic bullet put her back on track, but the development of friendships with colleagues who shared her goals and aspirations played a key role in changing her trajectory. Those work friends nudged Rebecca toward prioritizing her health. When she confided in her colleagues that she was going through a divorce, they encouraged her to move into the city, which would cut her commute time in half and give her more free time to exercise. She began to work healthier habits into small moments throughout her day, for example, by agreeing to walk-and-talk meetings with a colleague in a different division with whom she was collaborating. "We'll work while we both walk," her colleague suggested. At first she wasn't sure she could pay attention while she walked, but she found that being free from the distractions of her desk allowed her to stay even more focused. She added an hour of exercise while still connecting on their project.

She started discussing work with colleagues over lunch, but over time, their lunches became less formal. Conversation easily flowed from work to relationships, marriages, children, aging parents—and they bonded sharing their highs and lows. Those lunches became so important that each of her colleagues made it a priority to hold that hour of the day open, regardless of the other demands.

They rarely discussed getting in shape or losing weight. It was just the positive influence of being around one another that started to rub off.

"We were pushing each other to eat a little better, make sure we were eating salads and that sort of thing," Rebecca told us. "I lost probably fifteen or twenty pounds within six months of doing that."

The change in Rebecca's physical health was as much a result of who she was connecting with as it was her own will to change. The effect over time was profound. Rebecca now has a new partner who is a positive influence on her health. "We enjoy cooking together," she said. "Even if I had that moment where I was like, 'Hmm, I really want McDonald's tonight,' my significant other would say, 'No, we're not doing that. Let's make something better.' I can't even remember the last time I had fast food."

For most of us, our commitment to our physical health is one of the first things we let slide as microstress builds. We slowly drop activities that once were central to our lives, because we're just too busy or too tired. We might try to turn it around with an ambitious New Year's health goal—*This year I will run that 10K!* or *This year I'll finally lose that baby weight* or *This year I'll get back into tennis*—but our resolution rarely sticks.

When we fall short on a physical health goal, the usual response is to blame ourselves—*I'm too weak-willed; I don't have enough focus*—or we chalk it up to the demands of life: *There is no time in my day.* But giving up on prioritizing your physical health can have lasting secondary consequences.

In this chapter, we'll explain why relationships are so important to your ability to combat the physical toll of microstress. We'll explore the path to better health that ten percenters consistently take, and we'll share practical tips about getting on top of your physical well-being and staying there.

How Our Networks Affect Our Physical Health

Why would our social networks have such a powerful influence on our health and longevity? In part, it's the direct effect that positive social interaction has on our biology. Evidence shows that social interaction is physically healthy. Supportive connections with others benefit our immune, endocrine, and cardiovascular functions and reduce the wear and tear of stress on our systems.[1] People who have satisfying, close relationships with their family, friends, and community are healthier and live longer.[2]

Making this all a bit trickier is the fact that as we enter middle age, a time of life when maintaining a healthy, active lifestyle becomes all the more important, we tend to drift away from many of our connections. One study of networks and health shows an inflection point around the ages of thirty-five to forty, when a person starts to become less connected to people who provide them with motivation around physical activity and nutrition and who participate with them in activities that improve their health.[3] This time of life is, of course, when most people have extraordinary work and personal responsibilities, triggering wave upon wave of daily microstresses. If you've followed a typical pattern, at the time in your life when you most need to have connections that reinforce good health, you are likely to have fewer than ever before.

In the ten percenters, we saw something different. They don't go it alone, they weave healthy activity into their daily lives through their connections with other people. They simultaneously adapted their behaviors and relationships to diminish the likelihood of regressing to old patterns. They consciously pulled themselves away from connections or situations that triggered negative health choices and then formed positive, authentic relationships that helped them stay on track. Their commitment to their physical health became as much about sharing their experience and being challenged and supported by others as it was about reaching a number on a scale or time running a 10K.

In our interviews, we asked people to reflect on times when they were becoming healthier—whatever that meant to them personally—and then to share not just what they were doing but also the role of the connections that enabled them to improve their health. How did the very busy people we spoke with successfully integrate new habits into their lives and avoid

FIGURE 7-1

Driving positive health trajectories through relationships

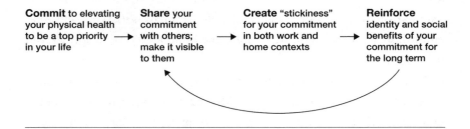

backsliding? Their answers produced a pattern that looked generally like figure 7-1.

If you reread Rebecca's story, you'll see that figure 7-1 represents the path she took to get herself back on track after years of letting her health slide. Each step leads to the next. Note that Rebecca's journey to better health took place in stages, not in one fell swoop. But it clearly happened through the relationships that helped her stay on track. Most high performers in this realm focus on how connections with others help build physical health through exercise and nutrition. But the same principles also hold for a smaller group that focused on wins around other physical goals such as mindfulness, meditation, sleep, preventive care, and stress management.

Let's take a deeper look at how each stage in the typical trajectory toward better health works and the crucial role that relationships play.

Step 1: Make Your Physical Health a Priority

Health typically becomes a priority when someone or something comes along at the right time and nudges us past our ability to put it off any longer. For some of us, we feel the nudge when a close friend or relative experiences a negative health event like a stroke, a heart attack, or a difficult diagnosis of something like high blood pressure. For others, it was a particularly bad day of feeling sluggish from drinking too much, or it was being shocked at the number on the scale in the doctor's office. And for still others, the nudge happened when someone in their network showed the benefits of prioritizing their health.

The push from other people is a critical part of the process. Connections help convert the abstract idea of improving personal health into a tangible and purposeful set of actions. Anyone can provide that final inspiration—family, friends, coworkers. And inspiration can also arise from negative sources, too. We might be motivated by the people we *don't* want to be like—the manager who becomes overweight and lethargic from too many business lunches or the colleague who looks exhausted and frazzled at work. One interviewee shared with us how his father had passed away after five years of illness, and he knew he didn't want his own sedentary lifestyle to eventually make him a burden to his children. In many cases, the combination of a new health priority and a personal connection work together to create the incentive for taking the first step.

Making health a priority helps us in three ways:

- **It programs our brains to act.** Once we focus our attention on achieving an important goal, our subconscious brain engages to help us succeed. Research shows that our neural pathways affect decision-making. When we set a goal, we are partly motivated to achieve it without realizing that our subconscious mind is actually driving the bus.

- **It reveals a range of negative thinking patterns that have kept us unhealthy.** We may look at fit people and think that we couldn't possibly achieve that. Or we may mistakenly believe that our bodies are somehow different from others' and that physical health is therefore unobtainable for us. But a genuine commitment to prioritizing our own health will often help us see where we're making inappropriate comparisons or engaging in negative thinking and spur us to actions that improve health.

- **Once we label something a priority, it's easier to allocate time for it.** It can be hard to justify starting your day with a half hour on the treadmill if you think only about how it will delay you getting to the work you need to do. Elevating health to a priority that is equal to, or higher than, other priorities was a consistent hallmark of all the people in our research when they described times of significant health improvement in their lives.

Clint, a senior leader in a manufacturing firm, reprioritized his health after minor surgery on his thyroid became his wake-up call. With a demanding job, the father of two was focused on work or family from virtually the minute he woke up to the moment his head hit the pillow. Squeezing in time with his family was always a challenge. Thinking about prioritizing his own physical health had seemed impossible. But thyroid surgery gave him a fresh perspective.

He wanted to recover swiftly, and he realized he didn't want to risk losing any time with his family in the years ahead because of poor health. Years of inactivity meant he had to begin slowly. He started walking— just short distances at first—but soon was able to go further. Of course, it makes sense that by starting with small efforts, Clint was able to motivate himself to initiate a journey to better health. But somehow, this time was different. He stuck with it.

His trajectory followed the same pattern that Rebecca's did. He first made his goal public, sharing with his family that he wanted to get back into shape. He created routines that helped him stick with it, such as not even looking at his email until he'd gotten a morning jog in. That way, he wouldn't get sucked into work microstress until he had taken care of his commitment to himself. And over time, he began to see himself a bit differently. He started thinking of himself as an energetic person rather than someone who crashed into bed each night exhausted. And with this reinforced identity, he allocated even more time to being healthy. He went from struggling through a morning walk to running 5K and 10K races on the weekends with a group of runner friends. "I just felt like I became a better version of myself," Clint told us.

Ten Percenter Tips

- **Shift priorities in multiple spheres.** Be deliberate about elevating health as a priority in every sphere of your life—work, family, friends, and so on. It's hard to make lasting changes if you target only one area of your life for healthier priorities while persisting with unhealthy activities in others. Clint coordinated his jogs with his wife, who arranged their schedules around this commitment and even provided gentle nudges (sometimes a physical one to get him out of bed) to get started and stay committed. He also made clear to his work colleagues that he wouldn't log on to his email until after he'd gotten his morning jog in.

- **Find role models.** Look around in your network to find people who have succeeded with, or are making good progress toward, their health priorities. Notice what they're doing and how it's affecting their energy and mood. A chance encounter with an old friend who was an active runner was what initially inspired Clint to give jogging a go. One person we interviewed was struck by how his manager told everyone that beginning at 7 a.m., she would be exercising and therefore unreachable for an hour. Also consider looking for anti–role models of people you don't want to be—people who have spent decades *not* living healthy lives and who are now suffering the consequences. This can be powerful motivation, too.

- **Elevate priorities that are genuinely meaningful to you.** Resist the common practice of judging yourself against those around you; the only thing that really matters is your own journey, not theirs. When David turned forty, he recognized that he had piled on the pounds in the past decade and was out of shape. Some of his college friends teased him about having a "one-pack" of stomach muscles instead of the six-pack he'd once proudly displayed. But rather than getting caught up in the goal of regaining his six-pack—which would have been difficult—he set a different goal for himself. "I wanted to be able to keep up with my son when we went hiking that summer," he told us. Having that focused goal helped inspire David to start walking around his neighborhood with a weighted backpack on weekends to get his body used to moving with some weight on it. Little by little, he improved his speed and distance and was delighted when he was able to match his ten-year-old son's pace on their summer hike.

Step 2: Share Your Commitment to Make It Visible to Others

We might be inclined to start our new health goal in secret, lest we slip up and people see that we didn't achieve what we set out to do. Resist this inclination. When family, friends, or coworkers know that we're working on a health-related goal, they will most often rally to our side. And in their presence, we are more likely to make healthier decisions. Goals that we keep private cannot generate this type of support. Even more powerful is a *shared goal*, which creates a side benefit of emotional and practical support from others. For many ten percenters, these interactions and relationships were what made the difference between persisting and sliding back. Over time, shared goals and public support help shift healthy choices so they become part of your identity. Sometimes these shared goals are significant endeavors like running a first marathon. But just as often they are small commitments such as walking together, attending yoga together once a week, or making a conscious effort to eat better.

We enjoy three major benefits from making our commitments to our health goals visible and sharing them with others around us:

- **We'll harness people's encouragement and emotional support.** Knowing that others are rooting for us increases our motivation to do the hard things necessary to hit our goals.

- **We'll naturally feel more accountability to live up to our commitments.** One person we spoke with wanted to improve the quality of her sleep, so she committed to her partner to leave her phone in the hallway at nine o'clock every night. The occasional frown from her partner was all it took to remind her when she tried to sneak in one last email before bed.

- **We'll often discover people in our lives who also want to get healthier.** This discovery opens new opportunities for us to exercise together, eat healthier food together, or engage together in other activities that enhance our physical health, strengthening our bonds.

William, a forty-three-year-old project manager in a large contract-services organization, never had time for exercise and never thought much about what he ate. He worked in an intense culture where people bragged about working weekends and late into the evening. A hard worker, he tried not to work late on a regular basis, but his days were filled with microstresses that drained his capacity. Because he had no choice but to let work spill over into nights and weekends, he often canceled plans with friends or ignored his personal priorities. He knew he was often irritable and coped with splitting headaches at work—the headaches disappeared when he went on vacation. Because William was slim, he assumed that he was healthy. He rarely went to a doctor, but once he did, he was shocked to learn he had high blood pressure.

When William mentioned his diagnosis to a few colleagues, they admitted to feeling similar effects from their all-in work culture. Together, they hit on a plan: de-stressing breaks. Instead of spending their coffee breaks sitting around talking to each other about work, they would leave the building for fifteen to twenty minutes and walk together or take a short drive to a nearby park with a lake and talk about anything except work.

The first few ventures felt silly and artificial, in part because they knew little about each other and their lives outside work. But over time, the conversations became more natural and evolved into deeply authentic connections. And it worked! Even these short breaks gave them perspective and improved the group's morale. And because these were group activities, people rarely skipped them.

After a few weeks, people noticed that they were more creative in the solutions they came up with and were more productive, too. Some of their desk-mates noticed the change in their attitude and wanted in on the de-stressing breaks. William and others helped different groups of people spin up their own tension-relieving breaks and lunches.

William's headaches and sleep problems faded, and his anxiety lessened. Yes, he still had lots of microstress on his plate, but he felt better able to prioritize his work tasks. He was also less irritable with his girlfriend. And his blood pressure began to go down even without medication.

You will struggle with staying motivated to improve or maintain your health as long as you see the effort as a solo one. Leveraging your relationships with the people around you to harness their support greatly improves your own ability to achieve important health goals.

Ten Percenter Tips

- **Be transparent with your goals or struggles.** The prospect of failure makes us inclined to not share goals with others, but we must be open about them if we are to create the community that will help us take an initial step and then persist in our pursuit of health. The sharing doesn't have to be a formal declaration, though it could be. Casually share in conversation that your goals will be hard and you need backup. Start with a limited circle of friends if that feels easier. One person subtly let others know about her goals with a calendar that she hung on her cubicle wall. She put a green check on the days she exercised and a red X on those she didn't. She wasn't sure anyone else even noticed, but just knowing that she'd have to make her progress public in this way was hugely motivating. Another person set a modest weight-loss goal and told his partner he would report on his progress at the end of every month. Knowing that the conversation was coming monthly kept his determination to succeed high.

- **Ask family members for help.** Families provide a particularly powerful kind of motivation through love and affection. One person told his family about his weight-loss goal and what behaviors he was cutting back on, like snacking during TV time. Even though his family only teased him playfully if he broke from his new habits (e.g., walking into the TV room with a bowl of chips), their response was enough to remind him to stay on course. Family members can also adjust their schedules for early-morning child-care, take turns going to the gym, or simply make an effort to pick up fresh produce on the way home from work.

- **Create group endeavors.** Public commitments are even more power-ful when they're shared among a few or many people. The group dedication instantly creates a support and accountability network. William's de-stressing breaks worked because of the group commit-ment. Another person we spoke with turned a commitment to biking into a group activity with friends, many of whom hadn't been on a bike in years. As the group grew stronger, the members began to incorporate additional recreational biking trips around town. Some even bought stationary bikes to train on during wet weather, and over time, the group pursued longer rides on their weekend trips.

Step 3: Create Stickiness through Relationships at Work and at Home

It's hard enough to commit to and initiate behaviors that improve your health. It's harder still to stick with them. Again, the answer to staying on course comes not just from willpower. It comes from your network—teammates who hold us accountable, family members who keep us honest about nonnegotiable exercise times, colleagues who celebrate our success, and true friends who are open to changing their own behaviors to support a change in ours. They form a web of support that prevents us from backsliding and feeds our ongoing motivation and commitment.

Creating stickiness around physical health goals can help in three ways:

- **Small decisions each day are no longer just our own decisions to make.** Stickiness means that when our motivation fades, there are people around us who will support and encourage us. This benefit isn't just about having someone to nudge us so that we don't skip our yoga class. It's about having someone we want to see at yoga class because doing yoga together—laughing through poses you haven't quite mastered, chatting before and after class, and feeling better as a result—has become central to building the friendship. Our decisions affect others, and we don't want to let them down.

- **The people around us remind us how good physical health can make us feel.** A positive role model—someone who reminds us that we're not our best selves when we let ourselves go or how good it feels to have more energy—can be powerful reminders of why our health goals are worth putting work into.

- **Stickiness gives us a sense of accountability toward others.** What we might not be willing to do for ourselves we will often do for the people around us—with the fortunate result that our networks help us show up and keep trying even when doing so is hard.

Inevitably, we found that stickiness relies on people who are open to changing their own behaviors to support a change in ours. They form a web of support that prevents us from backsliding and feeds ongoing enthusiasm and commitment.

James, who makes his weekly basketball game with friends a priority, knows that his teammates will give him grief if he says, "Look, I'm feeling kind of tired this week." They'll say, "We're all tired! You can still come out. Stop being a baby." He likewise dishes it out to his teammates when they're tempted to ease off. Stacie, who went from a sedentary lifestyle to running marathons, described the accountability that's formed when a person goes through grueling training sessions with others: "You can't be the one person who drops out with a trivial excuse. I felt the peer pressure, and it was enjoyable because you're all in this misery together."

Family members can often see us more clearly than we see ourselves and can help us recognize that not only does physical health make us feel better, but it also makes us better in our roles as family members, providers, and friends. James recalled that his wife would tell him, "When you get out of shape, you get grumpy." The husband of another interviewee would remind her that when she doesn't get daily exercise, it affects her humor and ability to focus, as well as her energy throughout the day. Those reminders add a sense of purpose that helps overcome the inevitable hurdles that stand in the way.

Ten Percenter Tips

- **Create nonnegotiable time.** Structure activities or priorities in your life in a way that even in the face of intense demands from work or home, you can still keep your commitments. James asked his assistant to help him keep his weekly basketball game commitment. "You can fly me wherever we need to go for business," he told the assistant, "but have me home on Thursday nights so that I can make basketball." For those couple of hours every week, he could count on leaving his work stresses behind and just enjoying the company and competition of his fellow players. As his stresses ebbed and became more manageable, his sleep improved. And James found himself able to rise above the microstress in his day a bit more easily. He told us, "I would listen to some new crisis and then calmly lay out how we were going to handle it, and people just nodded and did it. So much of the politics and infighting seemed to disappear. I think I come across as more authoritative now, and it helps people rally around my ideas."

- **See yourself with new eyes through your relationships with others.** A subtle difference for those who stick with their physical health commitments is how they focus on the positive aspect of their commitment, not just the negative of what they are trying to overcome. Their networks aren't just focused on helping them, say, lose weight, but also want to help them see the new sense of identity and positive changes they are creating—how they're creating a better version of themselves. For example, Shawn described to us how a loose collective of neighborhood dads who built a skating rink in one of their

COACHING BREAK

Managing the Negatives

Often, the people creating stress for us or enabling poor health behaviors are those we are closest to: friends, children, or spouses. Marriage, for example, is one of the most salient sources of support—but also a trigger for microstress for many people. And friends who are unhealthy can often bring us along for the ride and contribute to increased alcohol consumption, obesity, or poor nutrition decisions. Research has shown that if the people we are connected to are obese, we are more likely to become obese, too.[4]

Unhelpful behaviors in our networks are often as much to blame for our unhealthfulness as is our own will. We fall into unquestioned habits that are simply "what we do" together. The challenge of beating these negative influences is that we can't easily extract these influencers from our lives, because we love them, need them, or work with them every day. So what to do? We can alter the behaviors in our relationships with them. Try these practices:

- **Shift your interactions to positive environments.** Spend more time with people in situations that exert a positive influence—for example, taking a walk together—and less time where there is a negative influence, such as in restaurants and bars. This change might be hard if your relationship revolved around unhealthy behaviors; you may need to apply some creativity to find healthier alternatives. One person we spoke with thought that a long-standing Saturday morning get-together with friends at a pancake house would be hard to change. But after an honest discussion about his efforts to lose weight, everyone agreed to shift to having coffee on people's porches instead. After a few months, several people in the group admitted to being thankful for the request as the new approach benefited their health as well.

- **Ask others to adapt their behaviors, too.** It can be especially hard to commit to eating nutritious food if those around you aren't. And it can be difficult to initiate healthy behaviors in your life if others don't change how they interact with you. One person we interviewed asked her spouse to leave for work a half hour later so that she could get in a morning workout. Another person who lived in an urban setting drew a one-mile circle around their apartment on a map and asked his family to commit to walking to any destinations in that circle rather than asking him to drive them. Over time, the circle grew, and his family's walking habits made it easier for him to get the steps in that he needed.

- **Blend in healthier relationships.** Increase the amount of time you spend with people or groups whose health interests align more with your own. For example, one person we interviewed told us, "I always end up drinking too much when I go out with this one friend. Once we got going, it was hard to stop us. So, I invited another friend along who was more likely to call it quits after two glasses of wine. I was able to piggyback off their departure to make it easier for me to do the right thing." Or if your regular group of friends isn't big on exercise, find the group members who might be interested in being more active. Together you might get the group on their feet more, or if not, you may find new venues for the subset of friends who are interested in healthier activities.

backyards one winter became a great sounding board to help them each deal with a range of microstresses—new bosses, family tension around the holidays, sullen teens, and so on. They would chat informally as they built the rink, sometimes ribbing one another but always finding ways to offer support. Building the rink together— and in the summer, putting up volleyball nets and organizing informal matches—helped the members develop strong bonds.

On the surface they had little in common except living in the same neighborhood, but working side by side to build the rink and then being out there with their kids week after week helped connect them. They became an informal gang of buddies in a way that none of them had had since childhood. Shawn's family outgrew their modest starter home and could have easily moved a few miles away to a larger one in a fancier neighborhood. But he couldn't imagine losing access to the neighborhood dad group, and so instead of moving, he went through the more difficult and expensive process of building an addition to accommodate his growing family. "Seeing those guys every week helped keep my own problems in perspective," he told us. Because their shared activities always revolved around physical activities, each of them saw himself as part of a physically active group, reinforcing the desire to keep up with the group's activities. But the activity was never just about skating or volleyball—it was about developing authentic relationships with people who shared their passion or commitment.

- **Engage the people closest to you in healthy activities.** People often put exercise and time with family and friends in opposition: if we opt for one, we lose out on the other. It doesn't have to be that way. We can combine the two. One interviewee organizes nature walks with a few other parents from her children's preschool. Because they all work full-time, it's difficult to participate in some of the school events that bring parents together. But this way, they combine physical activity with a chance to get to know one another better. "It's an elegant solution because it hits that important time with friends, which is one of my priorities in life," she told us. "And time with family, which is another."

Step 4: Reinforce Your Identity and Obtain Social Benefits for Long-Term Commitment

Your self-identity is where healthy behavior gets locked in. Ten percenters are good at sticking to positive physical health behavior because over time, their connections and shared goals help them alter their own sense of identity—as a runner, a cyclist, a vegan, a mindfulness guru, or someone who stays calm because they meditate. When a behavior becomes part of who we are—and we embed this behavior in authentic relationships with others—it is no longer viewed as a tedious task to get healthy. In fact, some people's identities are so connected to a practice like meditation or yoga that they do with others that they won't feel balanced without being part of those groups every day. This sense of identity plays a direct role in helping us push back on the microstresses in other aspects of our lives. We don't allow ourselves to be defined entirely by work because there are other activities, ones that help us stay physically and mentally healthy, that we do with other people who matter to us. We have more in our life than that. Because ten percenters do not allow themselves or their energy and focus to be entirely defined by work, the slings of microstresses throughout any given day do not land as hard. This clarity of identity gives people the courage to push back on work and preserve time for activities that enhance their health. And it inspires them to look forward to showing up—for the activity and the relationships—in a reinforcing cycle that is much more sustainable than simply being accountable for a goal like weight loss. The magic lies in creating this positive pull and desire to be healthy, not just the social pressure to remove a negative like alcohol or weight.

There are at least two other reasons that harvesting identity and social benefits yield long-term commitment to health objectives and minimize the negative effects of microstress:

- **Long-term supportive relationships carry biological benefits.** In one study, researchers injected participants with a common cold virus and found that those with more effective personal networks were more resistant to the virus.[5] Positive personal interactions benefit our immune, endocrine, and cardiovascular functions, while low-quality interactions are associated with inflammation and impaired immune response.[6]

- **Activities help us form relationships with people different from us.** Because we naturally tend to surround ourselves with people like us, we're not prompted to question our goals in life, change how we think about adverse moments, or keep a positive perspective on what we have. Interacting with people who share a passion—a vegan lifestyle, swing dancing, or swimming, for instance—can help us bond with people from different backgrounds. These interactions can also open our eyes to new ways of looking at life. Ask yourself this question: When was the last time you were facing an issue and spoke to someone who saw it from a completely different perspective?

Connecting with others through athletic activities at work can also help broaden networks. Supriya, a director of engineering, attended a workplace boot camp once a week at lunchtime. She described the people who do sporting activities at work as having the best networks: "They have different tentacles that you wouldn't normally develop through your regular job." Other interviewees similarly described athletic pursuits outside the workplace as getting to know people who would never normally enter their social circle.

Ten Percenter Tips

- **Find kindred spirits.** Use your physical health goals to connect with people who share your passion but whom you might not normally interact with. Georgette is a hard-driving technology executive who after two decades in a high-pressure job downshifted to an individual contributor role. The change created an existential crisis for her. "I didn't know who I was anymore," she recalled. "It was the strangest thing. I used to be a very strong type A personality. I worked all the time. I always felt I had to do more, I had to go further, I had to save the day." Daily yoga introduced Georgette to a group of women who were supportive, not competitive. "It was so freeing to be in an environment where it was not only OK to be imperfect, but where we recognized the beauty in the failure. Thanks to yoga, I am more balanced now. I'm pretty good at saying 'I can't' or 'I won't.' I'm OK with my own imperfections and limits." Over time, the principles of yoga have become infused into Georgette's identity.

- **Be vulnerable with others.** Being open and vulnerable with people who are different from us can provide new outlooks on challenges at work or in relationships, and it can help us see the positives that we have taken for granted in our lives. We often heard interviewees describe how they formed new relationships, with deep bonds of friendship and trust, through the shared vulnerability of activities like training together for a grueling race or confessing weaknesses at a weight-loss meeting. Ana, an executive who trained with a group at work for a 100K charity walk, described how the people in the group were mostly new to the company and didn't know each other well. But the atmosphere changed as they struggled through miles and miles of walking together. "You could see people having their dark moments," she recalled, "and they would go quiet, and you would see the others having to pull them through." They learned about themselves and each other and how they respond under duress, and to this day, people in the group remain close.

- **Create space for relationships.** Make the effort to go beyond the physical health activity to engage with others. People often miss out on these opportunities by overlooking opportunities for conversations before and after events or exercise. Take a moment to strike up a conversation with people, and do so on two levels. First, talk about which part of the activity you enjoy or struggle with. Second, talk about what else is going on in your lives. Expanding the conversation in this way is a common first step that many interviewees use to develop deep friendships over time. As a working new mother, Ana, the executive who was training for the 100K walk, had not had a chance to connect with other moms in her community. But there were several mothers in her work's walking group, and she began to bond with them on the edges of their walks—before and after—discussing the challenges and joys of being a working mom. She also began to feel more confident in her work itself, knowing that a few of her colleagues were supportive and would likely have her back at work.

Prioritizing Your Physical Health

Here's how to jump-start your own physical health trajectory—and stick with it. Start by identifying a health goal that you'd like to elevate as a priority. It could be getting back into running, going to the gym, or losing five pounds—anything that's important to you. Then walk through the steps of creating visibility and stickiness, picking out the recommendations that work best for you and for the goal you've chosen. Reflect on how the planned changes will affect you in terms of your identity and the additional social benefits that are likely to come your way.

Equally important to what you actively do might be what you remove from your life. Ten percenters are successful with their physical health in part because they are able to manage negative interactions—especially with people who create stress or enable unhealthy behaviors—that might knock them off course. Table 7-1 shows how you might consider mapping out a plan.

TABLE 7-1

My top health goals: Mapping out a plan

Quality being sought	Steps	Examples	What you plan to do, and whom you will do it with
Priority	**Elevate physical health as a prioritity:** Pick a physical health goal that's important to you.	Go to the gym three times a week, improve your speed, lower your cholesterol, lose five pounds.	
Visibility	**Create visibility:** Who will you share your goals with?	Talk with spouse/ partner or family about it, sign up with a group of coworkers for an event, post in virtual forums.	

Stickiness	**Build supportive structures:** Are there ways to arrange your calendar or benefit from prearranged structures of teams or clubs? How can you support your goal by setting aside nonnegotiable time for it? Who will keep you honest about your commitment?	Ask your assistant to schedule twice-weekly sessions with a trainer, set a schedule for cycling with Peloton, setting aside Thursday night for basketball with friends, make plans for weekend morning walks with friends.	
	Establish a sense of accountability: Can you join a group or club or enter a program with others so that you feel accountability for showing up and supporting other people? What small decisions can you make that will deepen your connections with others?	Sign up for a race with coworkers, joining a cycling club, start a weight-loss program with friends, go for coffee rather than rushing home after a spin class.	
	Get two-for-one: How can you involve the people who are already important to you in your healthy activities?	Go hiking with friends, join a parent-child soccer team, go to the gym with your spouse.	
	Manage the negative enablers: Are there people who influence you in the wrong directions? If so, how can you manage those relationships?	Shifting the relationships so you spend more time together in ways that help you with your goals, rather than detract from them.	
Identity and social benefits	**Reflection:** How do you envision these changes will affect your sense of self? Will these changes expand your relationships in ways that benefit you personally or professionally? Will they help you create deeper and more authentic relationships? Give you fresh perspective?	Connecting with a greater diversity of colleagues by joining company boot camp or running a corporate challenge race together.	

The majority of people in our research confessed to placing their physical health lower and lower on their priority list as they aged. There just wasn't enough time in the day. But the ten percenters don't see it that way. For them, commitment to their physical health through relationships with others is part of their identity. They feel bad when they're not engaging in healthy behavior.

No one gives up on their physical well-being in one fell swoop. We let it happen bit by bit as we become overwhelmed with the microstresses that consume our time, energy, and emotional bandwidth as the years roll by. Prioritizing our physical health through connections with others is a powerful antidote to microstress. That, by itself, can provide us with a better quality of life. But the benefits of having a strong network of support extend far beyond even our physical health. As the next chapter will discuss, the connections in our lives can help provide us with something even more powerful. In our connections, we can find purpose.

Chapter 8

How to Find
Your Purpose

 KEY INSIGHTS

- People need to provide for themselves and their loved ones. **But consider whether you've fallen into the trap of going one step too far, working a little bit harder and longer to keep up with society's definition of success**—a bigger house, better cars, fancier vacations—and losing activities, relationships, and identities you once held dear.

- **When you have a strong underlying sense of meaning in what you do, you'll be more likely to reframe microstresses in ways that make them tolerable.** Purpose reminds you why it's worth hanging in there during rough patches.

- Despite common sentiment, **purpose is not found solely in the nature of your work; your relationships with others in and out of work play a central role in the meaning you find in your life.** It's not just what you do, but how you do it with others.

- **We have identified five *purpose generators* that you can inten-tionally build into your everyday relationships** without needing to completely overhaul your life:
    - Seizing opportunities to help others
    - Pursuing personally meaningful life roles and goals
    - Finding authentic connections in small moments
    - Cocreating with colleagues
    - Connecting through shared values

- **Purpose isn't found only in noble work or lofty save-the-world ambitions.** Ten percenters show how purpose can be effectively created through small moments of authentic connections with others in everyday life.

With his business trip canceled at the last minute, Marco had a rare day off from work. Because he had cleared his calendar for the trip, he had no pressing reason to go into the office. Most days, he was long gone from the house before his kids even woke up. On this day, he lingered in the kitchen, hoping to chat with them as they rushed around getting ready for school. But his children mostly ignored him. His wife had stopped to talk long enough to ask him about a few chores before she drove off to work. How should he spend this precious day off? A decade ago, he might have called a buddy for a game of tennis, but he had stopped playing after a knee injury. "This is pathetic," he thought. "It's a beautiful day, I have no obligations, and I don't have anything to do or anyone to call." He thought about just going into work after all.

As he wandered around his empty house, Marco had a wake-up call. As the years passed, he had incrementally deprioritized parts of his life outside of his family—things that had once brought him joy—because he was consumed with work. "There is a temptation to just let stuff slide over time," Marco told us. "It just kind of spirals. You invest an awful lot of yourself into work and your career when you're young and trying to climb the ladder. Then you have kids, which is of course wonderful, but you realize that between children and your work you don't have a lot of time to do things that are just for yourself." As the years passed, he had incrementally let go of those joyful outside activities in his life. His days were obstacle courses of microstress. Among many other activities, he had to assist his aging parents, who insisted on staying in their own home even though they were unable to keep up with the maintenance, and he had to learn the nuances of working with his third new sales manager in the past two years. He simply had no time or energy to do anything but push through the microstresses in his daily path. He settled for not being unhappy. But that, of course, is not the same as having a strong sense of purpose and meaning in your life.

In our research, stories like Marco's were legion. Head-down corporate climbers often woke up one day to realize they had drifted far from the life they had once aspired to. They typically flagged a "step too far" they had taken: a critical inflection point—a bigger mortgage, a longer commute, or a promotion that required more travel—that somehow changed the tenor of their lives. Their personal narratives became work narratives only. Something was missing. "I'm not the same guy I was in college," one lamented to us. "I've lost my spark."

Maybe you seldom think of purpose because it seems ephemeral or because it's something that you don't have the time to deal with. But that would be a mistake. A sense of purpose, however abstract the concept may sound, plays a critical role in your ability to survive microstress.

And purpose may be even more important as we age, say British researchers Andrew Steptoe and Daisy Fancourt, who have studied the connection between purpose and overall well-being: "Maintaining a sense that life is worthwhile may be particularly important at older ages when social and emotional ties often fragment, social engagement is reduced, and health problems may limit personal options."[1] With a strong underlying sense of meaning in what we do, we are more likely to reframe microstresses in ways that make them tolerable. People with greater purpose in their lives demonstrate greater capacity to regulate negative emotions—making it less likely that they will be dragged down by fears or anxiety.[2] They also find it easier to pick themselves up and keep moving forward in the face of adversity.[3]

But the benefits of finding and knowing your purpose stretch far beyond simply having a reason to get up in the morning. Research also shows that purpose contributes to a significantly lower risk of dying from a heart attack or stroke.[4] And a sense of meaning in life leads to better sleep and greater resilience.[5] There's even evidence that people with a strong sense of purpose live longer.[6]

Neuroscience is also revealing how a sense of purpose affects brain function. In one study, a strong sense of purpose was associated with slower responses from the amygdala—the part of our brain associated with fear and anxiety—and increased activation of the anterior cingulate cortex, which houses higher-level functions such as attention allocation, decision-making, and impulse control.[7] The implication is that a sense of purpose helps us tamp down fear responses and enables our more rational thoughts to take precedence, thereby allowing us to better manage stressful situations. Another study found that people reporting a greater sense of purpose in life scored higher on tests of memory, executive function, and overall cognition.[8] Purpose helps fend off microstress and makes you think more clearly. People with greater purpose in their lives demonstrate greater capacity to regulate negative emotions—making it less likely that they will be dragged down by fears or anxiety.[9] They also find it easier to pick themselves up and keep moving forward in the face of adversity.[10]

We saw the results of the neurological and physiological effects of a sense of purpose in our interviews. The people we interviewed who had a clear sense of purpose seemed to experience microstress differently. They didn't get caught up in minutiae as much as people whose entire identity revolved around work. They also seemed to make better trade-offs in their lives—like Matthew, the previously mentioned ten percenter who walked away from the half-million-dollar performance bonus that would have required him to relocate his family. These positive trade-offs accrued, and over time, people experienced massive health and well-being benefits.

Of course, knowing that a sense of purpose is critical to your well-being doesn't necessarily make finding your own purpose easier. Many of us are so consumed with getting through the daily struggles of life that we don't allow ourselves the "luxury" of taking time to find and focus on a worthy purpose.

But stick with us. If you're relating more to Marco, who found himself without anything but work, than Matthew, we can offer you hope. You can find your purpose, and it doesn't have to be through massive life shifts or experiences. In fact, the happiest people we interviewed excel at finding purpose in what you might consider the most mundane activities.

Purpose Generators in Your Life

Creating a sense of purpose through our relationships provides three specific benefits. First, it helps us persist in difficult situations because we see the broader reason to fight through tough times. Second, it helps us be more rational, despite the microstresses threatening to drag us into emotional responses. Neuroscience has shown that a sense of purpose slows responses that come from the fear centers of the brain and activates higher-level functions that assist in decision-making and impulse control.[11] And finally, purpose makes microstress more tolerable. It reminds us why it's worth hanging in there during rough patches.

In this chapter, we'll discuss practical steps you can take right now to start building purpose. We'll identify five purpose generators that you can intentionally build into your everyday relationships without needing to completely overhaul your life where you can find purpose through relationships in your life, whether it's in the workplace, at home, or in your community.

Seize Opportunities to Help Others

Giving to others even in small ways can generate a palpable sense of purpose. And that's not just because we've been taught that it's the right thing to do. There's actually a scientific explanation for why helping others gives us a sense of purpose. It's rooted in the distinction that researchers often make between activities that are eudaemonic versus hedonic.[12] Eudaemonic (from *eu*, meaning "good," and *daimon*, meaning "spirit" or "soul") activities are outwardly focused and include those in which we give of ourselves to others. The term comes from what Aristotle described as the "pursuit of virtue, excellence and the best within us."[13] In contrast, hedonic (meaning "pleasure") activities are focused inward and concerned with more momentary fulfillment. Getting the latest phone, splashing out on a gourmet meal, or winning a new sales contract may be hedonic activities. None of them are bad on their own. But when your life is dominated by pursuit of hedonic rewards, you can start to make choices that will not lead you to happiness in the long run.

Emerging neuroscience research shows activities that transcend the hedonic, such as giving to others, lead to greater well-being over time. In one study, functional MRI scans were used to observe neurological activity in the reward center of the brain, the ventral striatum, when the subject thought about either giving or receiving money.[14] In some people, questions about giving money (e.g., if you were giving money, whom would you give it to, and why?) stimulated high reward activity. In other people, questions about receiving money (e.g., if you were to get money, what would you spend it on, and why?) activated the brain's reward center. But over time, an interesting pattern emerged. When researchers measured depressive symptoms in each group one year later, they found that the participants whose brains had lit up from giving money experienced a decline in depressive symptoms, whereas the people whose brains rewarded them for receiving money showed an increase in depressive symptoms.[15]

In contrast, hedonic activities beget hedonic activities. Getting more material stuff makes us want additional material stuff in a feedback loop that researchers call the *hedonic treadmill*.[16] But the gains we feel from hedonic activity wash away quickly for two reasons: First, our rising aspirations mean we quickly become accustomed to our new clothes, car, house, phone, computer, and so forth, and seek the high of getting the next item. Second, social comparison keeps us on the lookout for what others have and what we hedonistically want, whether it's a big house, a desirable vacation, or an interview with a top organization.

The hedonic treadmill is fueled not only by material things, but also by societal expectations of who we are supposed to be. Even though the desire to become a perfect provider, parent, and so on stems from good intentions, the goal puts people on the same treadmill (as did the identity-challenging microstresses discussed in chapter 4). Just as microstresses that drain our capacity almost always set us up to fail—there are only so many hours in our productive days, and even a single microstress can cause ripple effects for hours—we are often setting ourselves up to fail by only noticing how we fall short. We minimize what we're already doing in our minds and beat ourselves up about what we're unable to do. We set the bar higher and higher, blaming ourselves when we fall short. The cycle of microstress is exhausting.

Ten percenters have the material trappings of success—they are, after all, recognized by their companies as high performers and are rewarded accordingly. Even so, material acquisition isn't the focus of their identity. Instead, their sense of purpose is separate from money, society's expectations, or other things, and that helps them transcend the pressures of hedonic lifestyles.

When leaders in our research spoke most passionately to us about their sources of purpose at work, their passion often involved a role they played in mentoring others. For example, a conversation with a new hire helped Natalia, a senior staff member in a financial services company, find novel sources of purpose through her work. Natalia was one of the leaders whom HR occasionally tapped to have a coffee chat with new hires as part of the onboarding process. She had a standard routine for these chats: she would describe her own career progression, discuss the company's merit-based culture, and then ask the new recruit a few perfunctory questions about his or her background. She enjoyed the chats, but she had always seen them as kind of a PR performance: establish herself as one of the more approachable leaders and thereby chalk up goodwill with the HR team, whose help she needed from time to time to deal with personnel challenges.

But when she had one such chat with a new hire named Jenny, she found herself more interested in Jenny's story than her own. Though she was in her early thirties, Jenny told Natalia that she had only recently graduated from college. She'd had children young and been late to find her professional path. Now a single parent, Jenny was elated to have been given an opportunity to join the company and didn't want to blow it. But the new hire was worried about balancing work and home. "I'd welcome any advice you could give me," she told Natalia.

Natalia thought she could make a real difference in Jenny's career. "I'd be happy to have these coffee chats on a regular basis," Natalia told her. "In fact, would it be helpful if I organized casual coffee chats that included a few other people? I think we probably have a lot to share as a group." Jenny jumped at the opportunity to develop a real relationship with someone she considered a role model. Meanwhile, Natalia saw a path to connect with junior staff members more meaningfully, rather than just command-performance onboarding meetings or periodic performance reviews.

"I suddenly saw my years of hard-earned experience in a new light," she said. "I never had the benefit of a real mentor, and I could see how valuable it was." Becoming so connected to some of the more junior staff opened Natalia's eyes to new things. The new people had different perspectives on work, different technology tools, and different ways to collaborate. She was learning from them, too.

Giving can take many forms. You could acknowledge someone's contribution, ask them how they are doing and mean it, show empathy, pass on a small note, or share an article. Even for young people who may think they have little to give, the simple act of asking someone to mentor you gives status to the person you're asking. Throughout our research, we found that too often people shut themselves off from the important benefits of giving, because they weren't thinking creatively or broadly enough about what they had to give.

Ten Percenter Tips

- **Seize unexpected opportunities to help.** Many of us can easily recall times we stepped up to help a stranger, say, carrying a heavy grocery bag in the parking lot, stopping to help a lost child find a parent at an amusement park, or even just witnessing a neighbor's signature for a document that they were anxious to get filed. In these moments, when we rise to small occasions, our assistance helps them with their microstresses and helps us too. It's the opposite of the cycle we initiate for ourselves when we inadvertently create microstress for others. In helping remove microstress for someone else, we boost our own resilience. One person we spoke with found herself helping an older man in line at a local pharmacy trying to book a Covid vaccine appointment. He was flustered by the process. She stepped out of line and took a few minutes to help him book his appointment. It completely changed her perspective on the myriad microstresses she was fending off that day at work. "It was just a small gesture," she said, "but it gave me such a boost."

- **Find purpose multipliers.** Ten percenters find time in their busy lives for purpose-inspiring connections by focusing on *two-for-one experiences*, choosing an activity that fuels purpose in multiple ways. When Alicia volunteered in the library at her kids' school, she knew she was serving a higher aim and giving to others. She got to see her kids at school and, at the same time, was demonstrating the importance of community service and education. A bonus was the camaraderie she enjoyed with other volunteer parents. As Alicia saw it, "These are the people that I like to hang out with socially anyway." She was able to hit three of her purpose anchors—volunteerism, family values, and friendship—with one activity.

- **Find purpose in small moments.** One executive told us that she kept going to choir practice week after week in part because one of her fellow altos told her she relied on the executive's superior music sight-reading ability to sing a new song. The alto made a point of sitting close to her at rehearsals so that the executive could help her learn new songs more quickly. Seeing our contributions to a greater good, even if they happen in small

Recognizing—and Handling—the Warning Signs of Purpose Killers

Look for warning signs that your interactions with others are microstresses instead of purpose generators. These include the following:

- **You can't see how what you do makes a difference; the why of your work is missing.** If you're feeling that you haven't made a difference, reach out to others to gain a new perspective. A sales rep might get a new take on her job after hearing from customers about how she adds value, or your spouse or partner might reframe your work challenges in ways that show your positive contributions more expansively. Start a conversation with colleagues, customers, or people close to you, and you may be surprised at how much value they see in what you do.

- **The company's values are out of sync with your own.** Perhaps your management talks about noble intent, but their decisions don't reflect that. If you're feeling this disconnect, don't try to turn the whole ship. You're not going to be able to change your company culture single-handedly. And you might not have the option of leaving for another organization whose values are more in line with your own. But company culture usually exists in microenvironments, with variations across different groups. Seek out the pockets where people's values

moments, can provide us with the motivation to keep going even when microstresses are threatening to bowl us over. The simple act of noticing and celebrating others' efforts can allow you to find purpose in small moments. You become the person who sees someone else; you validate their effort. At work, don't rush to focus on the next big problem or objective without noticing and celebrating effort and contributions. One worldwide study align more with your own. Do so by means such as working on projects that introduce you to people outside your own group or taking classes that attract a cross-section of employees. Another approach taken by some of the interviewees was to create a counterbalance to their work lives in volunteer activities outside work.

- **You feel as if nobody knows you beyond your work or cares about you as a person.** If you're feeling underappreciated or think others around you are, open up a little. Even if you're skeptical about bringing your personal life to work or you're an introvert, you can find safe ways to show your dimensionality. For example, one manager started each team meeting with two songs, one that appealed to the younger generation and one that appealed to the older. This practice prompted people to start talking about the songs and sharing more about themselves.

- **There's a lack of trust, or you feel unable to be your authentic self.** Trust can emerge organically, but it doesn't have to. If you think trust is missing, there are systematic ways to build it. Our research has identified ten behaviors that build trust. Among other steps, you can make sure your words match your deeds, clarify the boundaries of your knowledge, give away a piece of knowledge, and act with discretion.[18] Sharing these trust behaviors as a group can be a first step toward building trust into interactions that affect your sense of purpose.

conducted by Towers Watson found that the single highest driver of engagement at work is managers' genuine interest in workers' well-being.[17] The bonus is that becoming someone who actively sees and appreciates colleagues makes you feel good, too. It can be as simple as thanking a colleague for working late to finish a report or for volunteering to give you peer feedback on a presentation before you show it to your manager.

Pursue Life Roles and Goals That Are Meaningful to You

Too often we allow ourselves to fall into unfulfilling roles defined by other people's ideas of success or fun. In our research, those who found purpose in everyday life did so by defining the roles that mattered most to themselves—and then structuring their interactions with others in ways that supported those roles. Equally important, they also made a conscious decision to remove themselves from interactions that created microstress or pulled them away from how they wanted to show up in work and life.

Consider Evelyn, a lifelong runner, who defined herself through society's definition of being an elite athlete. For decades, she had measured success through personal best times. She shared this joy with others, but the group she shared with had become increasingly small, just a set of competitive runners she spent time with. With her demanding professional life running for competitive times almost always meant training in the wee hours of the morning—alone—pushing herself physically but without the laughter or resonance of being with teammates she had so valued in her college experience. And if she didn't have a personal record one year, then she beat herself up for insufficient motivation or training.

Eventually, she realized that personal records weren't that meaningful to her. They were someone else's idea of fun. Part of what she had once loved most about running was being part a team, both in high school and in college. That was the purpose she wanted to pursue. With this realization, she started running with her daughter, the daughter's best friend, and the best friend's mom. None of them could keep up with her when they started, but she adjusted her pace and distance to suit them.

The group of four evolved into an open-invitation running group for women. Running became the means to meaningfully connect with people Evelyn cared about. She found joy in mentoring their progress and spending time with people doing an activity that all of them loved. With this shift—she still considered herself a runner, but she was no longer running for status or pushing herself harder and harder—she found renewed purpose. This is the magic we saw throughout our interviews with ten percenters. They found ways to live life more richly—with others—by subtle shifts to *activities they were already doing*. They were enjoying purpose-fueled lives and not pushing the idea of a meaningful existence over the horizon to someday.

It is striking how clearly ten percenters can find and articulate purpose in everyday life. They found joy in sharing the small ways that they believed they contributed to the world every day. Their stories ranged widely. One leader at a biotech company very consciously wanted to show her daughter what it looked like to be an unapologetically successful woman. Another executive we interviewed found his higher calling in passing on the company's unique culture to the next generation. There was a manager who prioritized giving dignity to employees during a downsizing. And one investment banker we interviewed had no delusions of grandeur that raising money had a higher purpose, but he felt great meaning in developing his team. In all these cases, people found that defining and fulfilling life roles and priorities in relation to others and then deliberately creating activities that supported those roles—and removing themselves from those that didn't—gave them a profound personal sense of purpose.

Ten Percenter Tips

- **Seek positive—and negative—role models.** Think about the people you admire who seem to live their life on a higher plane. Try to identify how they manage to work purpose into their everyday lives. And just as you do with your physical health, think about the people you *don't* want to turn out like. One top consultant told us that he was struck by the retirement party of one of the most successful salespeople in his company. The retiree had given virtually every waking hour for years on end to the company but had no outside activities to retire to. He delayed his retirement several times until the company stepped in to enforce its mandatory retirement age. "I don't want to be that guy," the consultant told us. "He had no reason to get out bed except to make more money."

- **Remind yourself of who you once were.** Sometimes you may need to look to your past to remind yourself of the roles and priorities that once animated your life. Reignite a passion from your past, and use it to slingshot yourself into new groups. You can be the old you once again, even if it's with new people. One forty-something manager shared with us that she had recently started flying again. She had earned her private pilot's license in her early twenties, but as the years slipped by, she had let her skills lapse. When she realized how close her house was to a local private airport after a recent move, she decided to become part of a local flying club. "There is no better way to leave your stress behind than literally seeing the world from a different perspective," she said. But the real bonus, she told us, was being part of a group of flying enthusiasts again. She looked forward to her weekend mornings hanging around the hangar with other pilots. "I enjoy talking with them about flying. It's totally different from the pressures of my everyday life."

Find Purpose in Small Moments

We too often leave small moments that could create purpose unharvested, for two reasons. Either we suppose that purpose only comes from the big, noble endeavors, or we think it's OK to put it off, assuming we can do that purpose stuff a little later, when things get easier. (Of course, they won't.) In our research, happier people were more likely to see and capitalize on small moments with others, in the present. For example, by:

- Expanding a relationship by asking off-task questions and discovering others' passions, shared perspectives, or values

- Stopping to speak with a colleague or neighbor for five minutes rather than rushing on to the next to-do

- Being vulnerable in a moment and so spurring others to do the same

In these ways, people were able to build authentic relationships by finding small moments of connection with others.

The networks of those who seek these small moments are often responsible for the insight. A mentor, a spouse, a child, a spiritual adviser, or a coach will point to sources of purpose that a person didn't realize were there. Ted is a sales manager overseeing a team selling agricultural supplies. He is also active in his church and meets regularly with his pastor on church business. Every couple of weeks, the pastor asks, "How is it with your soul?" Ted takes these questions to heart, and his pastor's questions stay with him in his everyday job through how he approaches his job, seeing great purpose where others might not. "I view my relationships with my dealers, my relationships with customers who I help with their farms, my relationships with the sales reps that report to me as pouring something positive into other people on this earth." Ted's conversations with his pastor encourage him to figure out how he can use his talents and the opportunities afforded by his profession to improve the lives of the people around him.

Ten Percenter Tips

- **Resist an overstructured life.** With the pressures of juggling work and home responsibilities, you may have fallen into a structured life that simply leaves you no room for building nonwork relationships. They are the first things you let slide when you're under the gun. And somehow, they never make it back onto your to-do list. You have to fight against allowing that to happen. Krishna, for example, has made a conscious effort to go with the flow whenever he can, rather than overplan his life. "As an example," he told us, "next week we are going to a new restaurant in town. We just put this out to a list of thirty friends and said, 'We are going on Tuesday. Who would like to come?' And people we haven't seen in a year came out of the woodwork. Imagine the reverse if we tried to plan a time with just two other couples—first it would have been weeks out, given how busy everyone is, and second, we wouldn't have gotten the surprises and joy of reconnecting!" Never in history have we had a greater ability to shape what we do and with whom. Don't allow an overly scheduled life to deprive you of the chance to lean into the smaller moments in life.

- **Be present in fleeting moments.** A surprising number of pivotal events in our lives are born in small moments that are easy to miss if we don't stop to lean in. Be as present as possible and aware of how your current experience is meaningful for you and for others. This approach could be as simple as telling someone you believe in them. Josephine, a successful tech company leader, deliberately heightens her awareness when she interacts with her team. She asks herself, "Do you believe in your people? Do they know that? Do you empower them?" As she explained to us, "These are the moments that actually matter every single day." Other interviewees described small moments spent with kids, especially after being away on business travel; conversations with colleagues over a cup of coffee; or aspirations to be as present as possible throughout the day.

- **Find small moments to learn more about people in your life.** You don't have to find extra hours to get to know people better. You can create opportunities in everyday interactions with them. In conversations, take even just a few minutes to ask questions to expand your appreciation of who a person is. Try to listen without agreeing or disagreeing, liking or disliking, or thinking more about what you'll say when it's your turn to talk. Discover other dimensions of the people you are already interacting with. Joaquin described how he began to feel community in his new neighborhood through serendipitous moments with neighbors around his cherry tree. "My neighbors were out, so I walked over and gave them extra cherries, and that sparked a conversation. The little moments like that, when you get involved, solidify the neighborhood network and bond."

Cocreate with Colleagues

If you've ever been part of a team where you have each other's backs, connect with your teammates as your authentic self, and build off each other's ideas to create something novel, you know that the experience can be incredibly energizing and purposeful. In some ways, it almost doesn't matter what project you're working on; purpose arises from the dynamics of how you're working together, a process we call *cocreating*.

Cocreating includes an element of synchrony—a deep sense of trust, commitment, and rapport. *We are in this together.* It can also include a scaffolding dynamic, in which the aha moments emerge as people build on each other's ideas, taking them to levels of innovation that no individual could produce on their own. Cocreating adds value, both to our own lives through the deep relationships we forge in the process and to others' lives through the strength of the ideas that we develop and build on as a team. Small moments of working on something together create an authentic connection, a kind of antidote to the flood of microstresses that otherwise fill our days. We are individually and collectively stronger working on something we create together.

Carol, a manager of engineering projects, experienced the satisfaction of cocreation with her colleagues on a routine basis. She described the synchrony of colleagues laughing together, even under intense pressure. In one instance, her team got called to an emergency meeting late at night. Nobody, of course, wanted to be up at that hour dealing with a crisis, but there they were, on a video call from their homes, meeting to find an immediate solution. Carol recalled the episode: "And one of my colleagues wrapped himself up in a blanket on his couch and made a joke, and the whole call just erupted in laughter. And I took a screenshot at the time, because I thought, like, 'Wow, this is a special team, that when we're under stress, we can actually have a laugh.' When you're working with a team like that—that's purpose."

In Carol's experience, the synchrony of the team also involved a sense of commitment to deliver for others, a recognition of the members'

COACHING BREAK

Falling Out of—and Back into—Purpose-Filled Connections

In our interviews, we asked people which life or career moves had shifted them into or out of purpose-fueled activities and relationships. Reflecting on figure 8-1, people told stories of how they either found or lost purpose through decisions at some of the depicted inflection points in their lives.

FIGURE 8-1

Where have you found or lost your purpose?

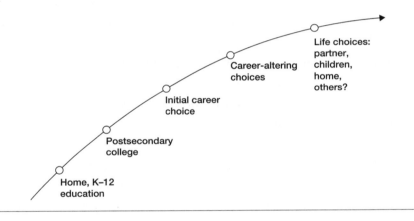

Life choices: partner, children, home, others?

Career-altering choices

Initial career choice

Postsecondary college

Home, K–12 education

sacrifices, and the desire to be worthy of those sacrifices. "When you look around a room at people who you have worked side by side with for thousands of hours, you feel responsibility to not to let them down. It's like, I know this person has given up Friday night for the last three years to do this patch process with us technically. I'm going to make sure that she benefits from that because I feel like that's a noble sacrifice, and I'm not going to screw it up." Feeling part of something bigger than herself—through authentic connections with a group of people—helped

Reflect on these inflection points in your own life. Does the process help you identify transitions that took you away from relationships or situations in which you found purpose?

Pinpoint ways that experience or activities at different points in your life have shaped your present connections—both those that fuel and those that deplete purpose. For example, people often mentioned pursuing socially desirable and high-income careers that took them out of activities and communities that kept them physically healthy or spiritually whole. In contrast, many also described inflection points like graduate school, marriage, or leaving a demanding job as critical to their moving into activities or communities that gave them purpose.

Identify opportunities to reignite past activities or dormant relations to add dimensionality and purpose back to your life. A common way most people reignited a sense of purpose lay with reaching back to passions or people that were once meaningful in their lives. Consider reengaging in activities like sports, volunteering, religion, music, or intellectual pursuits that could propel you into a new group of like-minded colleagues.

Carol shake off the microstresses that surrounded that work. "It doesn't really matter what you're working on at that point. It's just about, 'I like these people, and I'm not going to let them down because I'm part of this team.'"

Meanwhile, Carol's team was one she described as jazzed by how the members built on one another's ideas and energy to create a collective sense of momentum and creativity, where the whole was clearly greater than the sum of the parts. Think of the feeling many of us have when we look back at some of the best job experiences in our lives. Inevitably, they involve being part of a team that brought out the best in everyone on that team and the work itself.

Cocreating can happen in any undertaking—it's all about the dynamics of synchrony and scaffolding. Our interviewees described cocreating in the context of activities as diverse as building a new computational biology platform, working with a scrappy group of volunteers to launch a mindfulness program, and swimming with a local masters club.

Ten Percenter Tips

- **Embrace opportunities to get off task.** People who experience cocreation are often more open to solutions unfolding in unplanned ways. They have a general sense of what they need to accomplish but then focus on the why and the process of working together before diving too far into the tactics of when and how. It's OK to get off task sometimes to connect with your teammates. You can expand your relationships and understand people more holistically if you allow yourself time for questions and exploration, deepening your relationships with humor and fun. The trust developed in these interactions creates a solid foundation for genuine cocreation experiences.

- **Shift how you interact with colleagues.** Seek opportunities to work with colleagues on projects that offer you a sense of purpose. These occasions can be small moments of mentorship, collaborations with others who share your values or who offer you a chance to grow, or even volunteering to organize social activities with people at work.

- **Find purpose in unexpected growth opportunities.** Explore work worth doing and career alternatives at the height of your success. Ten percenters are comfortable making career changes when things are good, not bad. The momentum of their current role takes them seamlessly to the next possibility, which may be better aligned with their sense of purpose. One interviewee described his reaction after being offered a managerial position: "I never asked to be a manager, I never wanted to be a manager, I never thought of being a manager. And one day, I was in a meeting, and my boss at the time says, 'So, we want to make you a manager. You'd be great. Is that OK?' And I was like, 'What?' But you know what? I was actually a good manager. That gave me a tremendous sense of purpose that I never knew I would find."

Connect through Shared Values

Many of our interviewees described how their sense of purpose hinged on their ability to do the right thing—not because they had to push against a tide of pressure to do something else, but because they were part of a collective with shared beliefs and aspirations. The act of putting shared values into practice with friends, family, or coworkers can be a powerful source of purpose. Ten percenters find ways to connect through shared purpose, even when sharing might seem unlikely on the surface.

Josh, a senior leader at a manufacturing company, described how he felt a deep sense of purpose when he saw values triumph over personal interest. He described one of the company's guiding principles: everyone pulls together for the customer, regardless of the impact on individual bottom lines. "I don't feel like there are a lot of situations where it's my kingdom versus the sales kingdom versus the product development kingdom," he told us. "I think we're aligned on where we collectively need to be focused."

Josh had a different experience at another company. There, people would say that they would pull together, but that resolve disintegrated when it bumped against individual interests. He recalled, "People would say, 'Well, yeah, that might be the right thing to do but you're not taking it out of my P&L.' Or the salesperson is like, 'Hey, I got a quota to hit. I'm selling this thing anyway.'" Josh's experience is typical. Companies often drain employees of purpose by talking about higher aspirations but not acting on them. "At my former employer," Josh said, "I would go to the quarterly reviews, and it was twenty-five minutes of an old-school beat-down on the numbers. Did you hit them or not, and what were you doing to fix them? Now we have quarterly reviews, and probably the first five minutes are about the numbers. The other twenty minutes are about how we can do more for our customers and how we build our team and help it grow. Those are two discussions I never had before. Now, the numbers are our responsibility, but they're not our purpose."

One of the lessons we learn from ten percenters is that finding purpose in shared values isn't always as easy as Josh's experience. We cannot always simply find a company or culture whose mission or purpose we wholeheartedly agree with. That may not be realistic for many people. But you can find ways to connect with others over smaller moments. If you fundamentally prize being a mentor to younger employees, you might find other like-minded peers and organize mentoring efforts together. If you value creativity in your role or applying technology to solve problems, you can surely find others who value the same things and structure meetings or other interactions that fill this need for you. Those interactions can often start trajectories of work you find more meaningful. One secret of the ten percenters is their ability to mobilize people and create work streams around shared values. Over time, these efforts build momentum, becoming larger parts of their role or even the defining part. Put simply, ten percenters shape their circumstances and destiny through small initial investments rather than defaulting to always focusing on meeting others' expectations. In this way, they can actively sculpt their roles over time.

Ten Percenter Tips

- **Prioritize activities and relationships that create purpose for you.**
  No matter how clear you are about your purpose, you must have
  strategies for sticking with it when life is pulling you in many
  directions. Be methodical with your time. Use your calendar with
  discipline to make time for sources of purpose outside of work.
  "Even on the weekends, the things I want to make happen, like
  fun or social events, they go on the calendar," one busy executive
  told us. Rituals and routines help to hardwire purposeful interactions in your life. One interviewee volunteered at a local food
  pantry with friends one Saturday a month. Each friend worked

COACHING BREAK

Discovering Hidden Sources of Purpose

Use the exercise described in this coaching break to identify your existing purpose generators, to uncover gaps, and to find ways to extend your
sense of purpose through your relationships with others. The goal is not to
create an entirely new life plan but to recognize where you find purpose
now, to learn how to more consciously lean into those sources of purpose,
and to identify low-purpose activities that you might adjust or eliminate.

We'll walk you through this exercise using the analysis that we conducted with Meredith, a high-level media executive. Table 8-1 shows the
grid Meredith used. She initially told us that the primary purpose in her life
came from her roles at work (as a manager) and in her family (as a mother, a
wife, and a daughter). Each of them came laden with microstresses across
all categories. But when we asked her to work through this grid to identify her sources of purpose—or purpose-draining activities—she found new
insights.

Step 1: Extend existing activities to additional sources of purpose. Look
for ways you can add a new sense of purpose to something you're already
doing. This might be as simple as recognizing the value you're already
bringing to others through an activity and being a bit more deliberate
about what you do. Though she was clear about her formal role at work,
Meredith had given less thought to the informal ones, such as being a
mentor to team members at work. She started paying more attention to
this mentorship role, placing more deliberate effort into understanding the
needs and aspirations of her team members and changing her perspective
on things she found draining, such as performance reviews.

Step 2: Broaden your relational touch points. Find ways to connect with
more and different people through the activities you are already doing.
Meredith derived a great deal of satisfaction from the volunteer work

(continued)

TABLE 8-1

My existing purpose generators

To see where you might have opportunities to add purpose to your everyday life, start by recognizing what you are already doing. Then see if you can alter them or incorporate other people in ways that help you build purpose through these activities and connections. When Meredith fills this in, she sees sources of purpose that she hadn't paused to recognize, such as mentoring her team and teaching graphic design. But upon further reflection, she could also see how she could take those same activities and extend her sense of purpose through them.

PURPOSE GENERATORS	At work					Outside of work			
	Direct supervisor	Other leaders	Peers	Teams that report to you	Customers, clients, users	Spouse, partner	Family	Friends	Interest groups
Fulfilling life roles and priorities				• *Mentor team*	• *Client relations*			Recruit a friend	
Fulfilling a set of personal roles and priorities you feel are important to a life well lived									• *Teach graphic design*
Giving to others				• Extend sense of purpose	• Extend sense of purpose (not for profit)				
Using your time and talents to help others									
Seeing purpose in everyday life				• Extend sense of purpose	• Extend sense of purpose (not for profit)	• Alter a low-purpose activity			
Opening the aperture to see greater possibilities or higher purpose in what we do									
Cocreating							• Add a purposeful activity: Family tree		
Working together with synchrony (a deep sense of trust, commitment, and rapport and scaffolding (building on each others' ideas)									
Living shared values									
Putting shared values into practice with friends, family, or coworkers									

RELATIONSHIPS

she did, teaching graphic design. But she often felt that the time spent doing that came at a price to her friendships. The grid clearly shows a big white space in the "Friends" column. Meredith decided to see if she could engage some friends in what she was already doing, recruiting one friend to work with her on a volunteer graphic design project. Conversations around graphic design spilled over into authentic discussions around parenting and life in general.

Step 3: Alter a low-purpose activity. You might not be able to eliminate all the low-purpose activities in your life, but you can alter them in small ways that might make a big difference. The one part of her job that Meredith wasn't keen on was client relations. She loved the creative aspect of her work and seeing how ideas came to fruition, but the process of selling and negotiating with clients left her cold. The higher she rose in the organization, however, the more that client relations became crucial to her job. After talking it through with colleagues, Meredith decided to slightly change her client mix so that she'd be dealing with more nonprofits and other organizations whose work aligned with her values. These clients represented just a small percentage of her overall work, and they meant lower margins on sales, but she felt more kinship with her clients. What had previously felt like a hard-core selling became a process of using her creative talents to help others.

Step 4: Add a purposeful activity. Make deliberate choices to add one or two activities that you know you will find purpose in. They don't have to be huge time commitments, but they do have to be meaningful to you and connect you with others. Most notably, Meredith told us she had never really grasped how much she enjoyed cocreating. With these instincts she prioritized finding appropriate chances to collaborate in this way with colleagues. But the joy in cocreating extended to family and friends. Simply having a project to work on together created a bond. She decided to create an elaborate family tree with her extended family, with various relatives

(continued)

taking leadership roles at different points. By building on each other's work, they cobbled together a detailed history that finally included definitive answers on some family lore.

She made a point of taking time to formally interview each of her parents about their own childhood, recording the interviews. Another member turned those interviews into Ken Burns–style documentaries for the group. And Meredith set up shared Google drives within her extended family to ensure that everyone was up-to-date on the family tree. "It was energizing to recognize the good that could come from pursuing some of these other activities with people I care about," she told us. "It wasn't simply taking time away from my primary roles; [it was] extending them to be more inclusive and helping me see purpose in other areas as well."

After using that grid in table 8-1 for self-analysis, Meredith could see her collaborative activities not just as nice-to-haves but rather as need-to-haves because they were so important to creating and fulfilling her sense of purpose.

hard to keep that commitment not just because they cared about helping their community but also because they relished the chance to work side by side on something. They deliberately carpooled to get there, ensuring some time for social chat and to check in on each other's lives on the way there.

- **Vote with your feet.** Decline jobs or opportunities that would steer you away from your purpose. We repeatedly heard stories of people saying no, whether they declined work with teams that didn't share their values, jobs that would have made them more money but robbed them of time with family, or roles in which they felt obliged to work in marginally ethical ways. In some cases, they took their existing roles and reshaped them to be more purposeful. One ten percenter, for example, led the leadership development for his organization and created a model entirely based on mobilizing leaders to teach each other. "It wouldn't be as rewarding to me if I just ran the program myself," he explained. "So I've reshaped it to what I'd like it to be." Sometimes, people took on work they didn't need to take on but wanted to, such as a volunteer program around meditation, because it added meaning to their workday and ended up connecting them with people who shared a similar passion.

- **Lean into activities in new domains.** The happiest people in our research tend to be involved in groups in two (or more) of these four areas:

  - **Spiritual:** interactions around religion, music, art, poetry, and other aesthetic spheres of your life that put work in a broader context

  - **Civic and volunteer:** meaningful groups that create purpose and bring you in contact with a diverse group of like-minded people

  - **Friends and community:** collective activity such as athletic endeavors, book clubs, and dinner groups

  - **Family:** actions like caregiving, modeling valued behaviors, and living traditions and values with extended family

Marco, the previously mentioned executive who found himself with a free day and nothing to do, found a way to restore a sense of purpose in his life beyond work. He volunteered at a local environmental group to help clean up a park that had been overrun with trash and weeds. A wide spectrum of people of all ages and walks of life turned up for the occasional cleanup days, but Marco found that they shared the values of caring about the environment, a spirit of community service, and the fun of coming together on a Saturday to accomplish something. Little by little, he began giving more time to that group. And then he repeated this process with a local tennis group with his wife and a men's group in his church. Within a year, Marco had built into his life dimensionality and authentic connections that were deep sources of purpose and meaning to him. And this sense of purpose, in turn, allowed him to rise above many of the microstresses of his daily life—small things that had previously felt so important simply didn't have the same impact on him. "It may seem like such a small thing," he said, "but I think this has made me much happier at work because I do have some balance and a sense of purpose outside of work and my immediate family responsibilities."

Building purpose into your life doesn't need to come from deep soul-searching, in which you identify the reason you are here on this earth. But it does take intentional effort. As many of our interviewees discovered, daily life can sweep you up in invisible currents, pulling you toward the shores of societally defined expectations rather than the places where you find your personal values. Navigating the gauntlet of microstresses that drain your capacity, deplete your emotional reserves, and challenge your identity makes it even harder for you to find your way back. But if you wait until the perfect time in your life to allow yourself the luxury of finding purpose—perhaps when you have complete financial security or when the kids are fully grown—you may find that you've lost out on years of opportunities to build the relationships that lie at the core of a sense of purpose.

It's easy to get swept up in microstresses of the day without seeing any opportunities to create or follow a purpose in your life. But ten percenters see purpose differently. They don't create purpose in isolation; relationships with others play a central role. Purpose is not just what we do but also how we do it *with others*. Our relationships add dimensionality and perspective, helping us see the world more broadly and crystallize what really matters to us. In fact, many of us find that those relationships are what matters most to us. Things worth doing become more purposeful when they are carried out in collaboration with others who share common values. They remind us of who we are—or can be—when we're at our best.

CONCLUSION

Think Small

"We play a mix of stuff—from classic rock to some of the newer stuff that my bandmates are into," Peter told us proudly. "I've even had a couple of killer guitar solos."

Perhaps no one in our research was more surprised by the effect of small changes in his life than Peter, a highly successful neurosurgeon who found himself playing guitar in his mid-forties with a group of twenty-year-olds. Peter didn't set out to join a local band, but that's where he ended up after taking a series of small steps to try to resume an activity he had loved before his career consumed him. After frequenting a local music store to tune up his old guitar and buy some new music, he noticed a flyer looking for people who wanted to play in a low-key weekend band. "What we lack in talent, we make up for in volume!" the ad read. On a whim, he decided to respond. "It's completely different from surgery," he explained, "where I have to get in my head and stay totally focused. When I'm playing with the guys, I'm not in my head at all. I just let go. It's so much fun."

It had been many years since Peter thought of himself as a musician. But when we interviewed him, he was brimming with enthusiasm. What had made him answer that ad? we asked. "I just remembered how much I used to love being in a band," he said. "I just wanted to feel that way again."

Many of us have vibrant memories of ourselves when we felt we were at our best—maybe in college or in our early career years. But like Peter, we find that, little by little, the microstresses of our daily lives beat that kind of joy out of us. And we just accept that fate, bracing ourselves to cope with the ever-increasing battering of microstresses. Or we turn to conventional advice on improving our well-being—advice that tends to focus on what we can do to steel ourselves from stress (macro or micro), such as meditation or gratitude. These approaches focus on helping you create a better perspective so that you can tolerate more and more microstress in your life.

Wouldn't it be better if you could instead remove some of the microstress, rather than build up your ability to tolerate it? Decades of social science research suggests that a negative interaction has up to five times more impact than a positive one. All of us are flooded daily with microstresses that we don't even recognize. Think of the impact you can have by identifying and correcting even just one or two microstresses in your everyday life. Better still, think of the effect of creating some new, positive interactions with people who will add purpose and growth to your life.

In this book, we've given you the tools to identify the invisible ways that microstress is invading your life and the language to articulate what you're feeling. You can't fix a problem you don't know you have; you can't work on something you can't name. We have offered you tools and coaching breaks to help you diagnose where your microstress is coming from and suggestions for how to push back. But we have also asked you to pause for self-reflection about where you are inadvertently perpetuating the cycle of microstress, too.

We've shared with you here what the happiest people in our research do differently. Not only are they exceptional at deflecting and eliminating the microstress in their lives without sacrificing their performance at work, but they have also deliberately built and maintained rich, multidimensional lives. We have come to deeply admire the ten percenters who, like Peter, found ways to structure their lives so that they were fueled by interactions with others. Throughout our research, the two of us began to adopt some of the best practices we saw, both in recognizing and pushing back on the microstresses in our own lives and in finding micromoments of authentic connections with others. One of us (Rob) has reached back into a handful of pursuits from his past, including tennis and cycling, to establish a whole new set of connections that have become a source of advice, perspective, joy, and friendship he enjoys daily. And the other (Karen) realized that she had drifted from some of her closest friends from college even though they lived within an hour's drive. During even the roughest days of the pandemic, they made a point of meeting up on local hiking trails, logging miles side by side while allowing themselves to (at least temporarily) forget about the microstresses awaiting them back home. Over the months (and years) of the pandemic, the hikes have morphed into an even deeper connection as Karen and her friends supported one another through the challenges of moving homes, aging parents, health concerns, and empty nests. Their hikes have turned into frequent texts, gatherings at one another's homes, a special girls-only vacation together, and endless hours of laughter. Both of us have reminded ourselves of the power of having authentic connections with people we care about to help us keep our own microstresses at bay.

In decades of research, working closely with some of the world's most respected organizations and hundreds of high performers, we have never been so moved by the lessons we learned from the people we interviewed for this book. To be sure, there is a palpable crisis of well-being today. But there's also a powerful solution. Eliminate some microstresses in your life, and look for micromoments of authentic connections with others that will add new dimensions to your life. The reality is, we've never had more ability to shape what we do and whom we do it with. Start by thinking small.

NOTES

Introduction

1. Gallup, *State of the Global Workplace: 2022 Report* (Washington, DC: Gallup, 2022).

Chapter 1

1. Identifying details of people mentioned in this book have been disguised.

2. Lisa Feldman Barrett, *7½ Lessons about the Brain* (Boston: Mariner Books, 2020).

3. Janice K. Kiecolt-Glaser, Diane L. Habash, Christopher P. Fagundes, Rebecca Andridge, Juan Peng, William B. Malarkey, and Martha A. Belury, "Daily Stressors, Past Depression, and Metabolic Responses to High-Fat Meals: A Novel Path to Obesity," *Biological Psychiatry* 77, no. 7 (2015): 653–660.

4. Janice K. Kiecolt-Glaser, Christopher P. Fagundes, Rebecca Andridge, Juan Peng, William B. Malarkey, Diane L. Habash, and Martha A. Belury, "Depression, Daily Stressors and Inflammatory Responses to High-Fat Meals: When Stress Overrides Healthier Food Choices" *Molecular Psychiatry* 22, no. 3 (2017): 476–482.

Chapter 3

1. University of Nottingham, "Yawning: Why Is It So Contagious and Why Should It Matter?," *ScienceDaily*, August 31, 2017, https://www.sciencedaily.com/releases /2017/08/170831123031.htm.

2. Howard S. Friedman and Ronald E. Riggio, "Effect of Individual Differences in Nonverbal Expressiveness on Transmission of Emotion," *Journal of Nonverbal Behavior* 6 (1981): 96–104, https://link.springer.com/article/10.1007/BF00987285?LI=true.

3. Veronika Engert, Franziska Plessow, Robert Miller, Clemens Kirschbaum, and Tania Singer, "Cortisol Increase in Empathic Stress Is Modulated by Emotional Closeness and Observation Modality," *Psychoneuroendocrinology* 45 (2014): 192–201, https://www.sciencedirect.com/science/article/abs/pii/S0306453014001243.

Chapter 5

1. Harvard Study of Adult Development, accessed October 20, 2022, https://www .adultdevelopmentstudy.org/.

2. Liz Mineo, "Good genes are nice, but joy is better," *Harvard Gazette*, April 11, 2017, https://news.harvard.edu/gazette/story/2017/04/over-nearly-80-years -harvard-study-has-been-showing-how-to-live-a-healthy-and-happy-life/.

3. Daniel A. Cox, "The State of American Friendship: Change, Challenges, and

Loss," *Survey Center on American Life*, June 8, 2021, https://www.americansurveycenter
.org/research/the-state-of-american-friendship-change-challenges-and-loss.

4. Joel Salinas, Adrienne O'Donnell, Daniel J. Kojis, Matthew P. Pase, Charles DeCarli, Dorene M. Rentz, Lisa F. Berkman, Alexa Beiser, and Sudha Seshadri, "Association of Social Support with Brain Volume and Cognition," *JAMA Network Open* 4, no. 11 (August 2, 2021) https://pubmed.ncbi.nlm.nih.gov/34398201/.

Chapter 6

1. Ludmila Kašpárková, Martin Vaculík, Jakub Procházka, and Wilmar B. Schaufeli, "Why Resilient Workers Perform Better: The Roles of Job Satisfaction and Work Engagement," *Journal of Workplace Behavioral Health* 33, no. 1 (2018): 43–62, doi:10.1080/15555240.2018.1441719; Al Siebert, *The Resiliency Advantage: Master Change, Thrive under Pressure, and Bounce Back from Setbacks* (San Francisco: Berrett-Koehler Publishers, 2005).

2. On demanding jobs, see Barbara L. Fredrickson, "The Role of Positive Emotions in Positive Psychology: The Broaden-and-Build Theory of Positive Emotions," *American Psychologist* 56, no. 3 (2001): 218–226, doi:10.1037//0003-066x.56.3.218. On economic hardships, see Robert Brooks and Sam Goldstein, *The Power of Resilience: Achieving Balance, Confidence, and Personal Strength in Your Life* (New York: McGraw-Hill Education, 2004).

3. Deniz D. Polat and Murat İskender, "Exploring Teachers' Resilience in Relation to Job Satisfaction, Burnout, Organizational Commitment and Perception of Organizational Climate," *International Journal of Psychology and Education Studies* 5, no. 3 (2018): 1–13, doi:10.17220/ijpes.2018.03.001; Andrew Shatté, Adam Perlman, Brad Smith, and Wendy D. Lynch, "The Positive Effect of Resilience on Stress and Business Outcomes in Difficult Work Environments," *Journal of Occupational and Environmental Medicine* 59, no. 2 (2017): 135–140, doi:10.1097
/JOM.0000000000000914.

4. On physical or mental illness during challenging times, see Al Siebert, *The Resiliency Advantage* (Oaklander, CA: Berrett-Koehler Publishers, 2005); Polat et al., "Exploring Teachers' Resilience." On work satisfaction, see Robin Brown, Howard Wey, and Kay Foland, "The Relationship among Change Fatigue, Resilience, and Job Satisfaction of Hospital Staff Nurses," *Journal of Nursing Scholarship* 50, no. 3 (2018): 306–313, doi.org/10.1111/jnu.12373; and Zhimin Zheng, Poornima Gangaram, Huiting Xie, Stephanie Chua, Samantha B. C. Ong, and Sioh E. Koh, "Job Satisfaction and Resilience in Psychiatric Nurses: A Study at the Institute of Mental Health, Singapore," *International Journal of Mental Health Nursing* 26, no. 6 (2017): 612–619, doi:https://doi.org/10.1111/inm.12286.

5. Carol Gorelick, Kurt April, and Nick Milton, *Performance through Learning: Knowledge Management in Practice* (Boston: Elsevier Butterworth-Heinemann, 2004).

6. Janet M. Gibson, "Laughing Is Good for Your Mind and Your Body: Here's What the Research Shows," *Conversation*, November 23, 2020, https://theconversation.com
/laughing-is-good-for-your-mind-and-your-body-heres-what-the-research-shows-145984.

7. Don L. F. Nilsen and Alleen P. Nilsen, *The Language of Humor: An Introduction* (New York: Cambridge University Press, 2018).

8. Jan Packer, "Taking a Break: Exploring the Restorative Benefits of Short Breaks and Vacations," *Annals of Tourism Research Empirical Insights* 2, no. 1 (2021): 100006, doi:10.1016/j.annale.2020.100006.

Chapter 7

1. Shatté et al., "The Positive Effect of Resilience," Polat and İskender, "Exploring Teachers' Resilience."

2. Janet M. Torpy, Cassio Lynm, and Richard M. Glass, "Chronic Stress and the Heart," *JAMA* 298, no. 14 (2007): 1722–1722, doi:10.1001/jama.298.14 .1722; H. M. van Praag, "Can Stress Cause Depression?" *Progress in Neuro-Psychopharmacology and Biological Psychiatry* 28, no. 5 (2004): 891–907, doi:10.1016/j.pnpbp.2004.05.031.

3. George A. Bonanno, Camille B. Wortman, Darrin R. Lehman, Roger G. Tweed, Michelle Haring, John Sonnega, Deborah Carr, and Randolph M. Nesse, "Resilience to Loss and Chronic Grief: A Prospective Study from Preloss to 18-Months Post-loss," *Journal of Personality and Social Psychology* 83, no. 5 (2002): 1150–1164, doi:10.1037/0022-3514.83.5.1150.

4. Nicholas A. Christakis and James H. Fowler, "The Spread of Obesity in a Large Social Network over 32 Years," *New England Journal of Medicine* 357, no. 4 (2007): 370–379, doi:10.1056/NEJMsa066082.

5. Sheldon Cohen, William J. Doyle, David P. Skoner, Bruce S. Rabin, and Jack M. Gwaltney, "Social Ties and Susceptibility to the Common Cold," *JAMA* 277, no. 2 (1997): 5.

6. Teresa E. Seeman, Burton H. Singer, Carol D. Ryff, Gayle Dienberg Love, and Lené Levy-Storms, "Social Relationships, Gender, and Allostatic Load across Two Age Cohorts," *Psychosomatic Medicine* 64, no. 3 (2002): 395–406; Bert N. Uchino, *Social Support and Physical Health: Understanding the Health Consequences of Relationships* (New Haven, CT: Yale University Press, 2004).

Chapter 8

1. Andrew Steptoe and Daisy Fancourt, "Leading a Meaningful Life at Older Ages and Its Relationship with Social Engagement, Prosperity, Health, Biology, and Time Use," *Proceedings of the National Academy of Sciences* 116, no. 4 (2019): 1207–1212, https://www.pnas.org/doi/abs/10.1073/pnas.1814723116.

2. Fei Li, Jieyu Chen, Lin Yu, Yuan Jing, Pingping Jiang, Xiuqiong Fu, Shengwei Wu, Xiaomin Sun, Ren Luo, Hiuyee Kwan, Xiaoshan Zhao, and Yanyan Liu, "The Role of Stress Management in the Relationship between Purpose in Life and Self-Rated Health in Teachers: A Mediation Analysis," *International Journal of Environmental Research and Public Health* 13, no. 7 (2016), doi:10.3390/ijerph13070719; Stacey M. Schaefer, Jennifer Morozink Boylan, Carien M. van Reekum, Regina C. Lapate, Catherine J. Norris, Carol D. Ryff, and Richard J. Davidson, "Purpose in Life Predicts Better Emotional Recovery from Negative Stimuli," *PLOS ONE* 8, no. 11 (2013): e80329, doi:10.1371/journal.pone.0080329.

3. Stuart Taylor, "Building Your Resilience and Understanding Your Purpose," *SmartCompany*, October 9, 2017, https://www.smartcompany.com.au/people-human -resources/wellbeing/building-resilience-understanding-purpose.

4. Eric S. Kim, Jennifer K. Sun, Nansook Park, and Christopher Peterson, "Purpose in Life and Reduced Incidence of Stroke in Older Adults: 'The Health and Retirement Study,'" *Journal of Psychosomatic Research* 74, no. 5 (2013): 427–432, doi:10.1016/j.jpsychores.2013.01.013; Randy Cohen, Chirag Bavishi, and Alan Rozanski, "Purpose in Life and Its Relationship to All-Cause Mortality and Cardiovascular Events: A Meta-Analysis," *Psychosomatic Medicine* 78, no. 2 (2016): 122–133, doi:10.1097/PSY .0000000000000274.

5. On better sleep, see Eric S. Kim, Shelley D. Hershner, and Victor J. Strecher, "Purpose in Life and Incidence of Sleep Disturbances," *Journal of Behavioral Medicine* 38, no. 3 (2015): 590–597, doi:10.1007/s10865-015-9635-4; and Arlener D. Turner, Christine E. Smith, and Jason C. Ong, "Is Purpose in Life Associated with Less Sleep Disturbance in Older Adults?" *Sleep Science Practice* 1, no. 1 (2017): 14, doi:10.1186 /s41606-017-0015-6. On greater resilience, see Li et al., "The Role of Stress Management"; and Kayla Isaacs, Natalie P. Mota, Jack Tsai, Ilan Harpaz-Rotem, Joan M. Cook,

Paul D. Kirwin, John H. Krystal, Steven M. Southwick, and Robert H. Pietrzak, "Psychological Resilience in U.S. Military Veterans: A 2-Year, Nationally Representative Prospective Cohort Study," *Journal of Psychiatric Research* 84 (2017): 301–309, doi:10.1016/j.jpsychires.2016.10.017.

6. Patrick L. Hill and Nicholas A. Turiano, "Purpose in Life as a Predictor of Mortality across Adulthood," *Psychological Science* 25, no. 7 (2014): 1482–1486, doi:10.1177/0956797614531799.

7. Carien M. van Reekum, Heather L. Urry, Tom Johnstone, Marchell E. Thurow, Corrina J. Frye, Cory A. Jackson, Hillary S. Schaefer, Andrew L. Alexander, and Richard J. Davidson, "Individual Differences in Amygdala and Ventromedial Prefrontal Cortex Activity Are Associated with Evaluation Speed and Psychological Well-Being," *Journal of Cognitive Neuroscience* 19, no. 2 (2007): 237–248, doi:10.1162/jocn .2007.19.2.237.

8. Nathan A. Lewis, Nicholas A. Turiano, Brennan R. Payne, and Patrick L. Hill, "Purpose in Life and Cognitive Functioning in Adulthood," *Aging, Neuropsychology, and Cognition* 24, no. 6 (2017): 662–671, doi:10.1080/13825585.2016.1251549.

9. Li et al., "The Role of Stress Management"; Schaefer et al., "Purpose in Life Predicts."

10. Taylor, "Building Your Resilience."

11. van Reekum et al., "Individual Differences in Amygdala."

12. Veronica Huta and Alan S. Waterman, "Eudaimonia and Its Distinction from Hedonia: Developing a Classification and Terminology for Understanding Conceptual and Operational Definitions," *Journal of Happiness Studies* 15 (2014): 1425–1456, doi:10.1007/s10902-013-9485-0.

13. Huta and Waterman, "Eudaimonia."

14. Eva H. Telzer, Andrew J. Fuligni, Matthew D. Lieberman, and Adriana Galván, "Neural Sensitivity to Eudaimonic and Hedonic Rewards Differentially Predict Adolescent Depressive Symptoms over Time," *Proceedings of the National Academy of Sciences* 111, no. 18 (2014): 6600–6605, doi:10.1073/pnas.1323014111.

15. Telzer et al., "Neural Sensitivity to Eudaimonic and Hedonic Rewards."

16. Campbell Brickman, "Hedonic Relativism and Planning the Good Society," in *Adaptation Level Theory: A Symposium*, ed. M. H. Apley, 287–302 (New York: Academic Press, 1971).

17. Tony Schwartz, "New Research: How Employee Engagement Hits the Bottom Line," hbr.org, November 8, 2012, https://hbr.org/2012/11/creating-sustainable -employee.

18. Rob Cross, Amy Edmondson, and Wendy Murphy, "A Noble Purpose Alone Won't Transform Your Company," *MITSloan*, December 10, 2019, https://sloanreview .mit.edu/article/a-noble-purpose-alone-wont-transform-your-company.

INDEX

ACKNOWLEDGMENTS

I am deeply indebted to all the people and organizations associated with the Connected Commons, the consortium I cofounded as a way to help advance practical applications of network research in today's hyperconnected world.

The idea for this book emerged from work we were doing in the Connected Commons, studying the networks of high performers across hundreds of organizations. I was fortunate to have sponsoring members of the consortium push me to think about individual success not just as high performance but also as well-being throughout one's career. These foresighted people were thinking about well-being way before it became trendy during the Covid pandemic. I am extremely grateful for their vision and for the access they afforded to their organizations—allowing us to conduct large-scale quantitative network analyses and to interview more than three hundred executives. I am equally grateful to all those interviewees for letting me into the pains and joys of the personal and professional relationships that constituted their world.

Though there are far too many people to mention by name (please forgive me!), I would like to thank several individuals who had a significant impact on this work. First, Jean Singer was an amazing collaborator and coauthor in aspects of this research. Her influence can be seen in the thoughtfulness and depth of our findings—thank you, Jean, for contributing your time, intellect, and humor to this work! Similarly, Greg Pryor has been a constant source of intellectual contribution and pragmatic application of the ideas in this book. The work is both more creative and practical on many levels as a product of Greg's contributions.

Peter Amidon, Michael Arena, Mike Benson, Inga Carboni, Vinnie DiSalvo, Chris Ernst, Rebecca Garau, Peter Gray, Karen Kocher, Andrew Parker, and Deb Zehner have been similarly important to the evolution of this work through many interactions. My thanks also go to Danna Greenberg, my Babson colleague, who partnered with us on the resilience aspects of this research and urged me to pursue this research from the beginning.

On an institutional level, I am indebted to Babson College and many academic colleagues who see the value in rigorous applied research and have created space and support for this work. I am also deeply grateful for the partnership with the Institute for Corporate Productivity (i4cp) and the entire team there. Although there are too many to name, I would like to specifically thank Carrie Bevis, Madeline Borkin, Kevin Martin, Kevin Oakes, Kevin Osborne, Erik Samdahl, and Mark Walker for their support of this work. I also thank the Innovation Resource Center for Human Resources (IRC4HR), and in particular Jodi Starkman and Hal Burlingame, for their belief in the early stages of this work.

Many thanks also go to the editorial team at Harvard Business Review Press. In particular, this work has benefited significantly by having two amazing editors—Scott Berinato and Susan Francis—engage tirelessly throughout the development of the book. Each has had a major impact on this work on all levels—thanks to both of you for investing your time and intellect to make this book a success.

And finally, I thank my amazing children—Connor and Rachel. So much of what I have learned in this research I see reflected in your lives as you seek to live on your terms in ways that make me so very proud of and happy for you every day. You are my inspiration and guiding light as I look to engage intentionally and purposefully in life. Thank you!

—Rob Cross

When Rob first approached me about collaborating with him on this book, my days were already so busy that the idea was almost impossible to contemplate. How could I find time to work on a new book? I was, in fact, so busy, that I told him I could only meet if he came to the coffee shop that was within walking distance from my home. Meeting there would save me wasted minutes in traffic. Fortunately, Rob didn't consider the minutes that I was therefore asking him to waste to get there a deal-breaker. As he shared with me the insights from his research, his observations really hit home with me. I recognized that my own life was pulsing with microstress. And I had almost let it stop me from exploring what turned out to be a wonderful opportunity to cocreate something meaningful with Rob. I'm so grateful that you came all the way to Brookline that day, Rob! Working on this book through the pandemic reminded me of the importance of pushing ourselves to both build and maintain multidimensional lives.

Throughout this project, I began to consciously adopt some of the practices we have outlined in the book—most notably, making more time for friends who had unintentionally slipped down my priorities list. I won't let that happen again. My friends became an extraordinarily important antidote to the microstresses of the pandemic. And so I want to single a few of them out here.

To Laurie Flowers and Laura O'Keefe, thanks for the hours of walking and talking throughout the pandemic. Neither subfreezing temperatures nor masks obscuring our smiles could diminish the joy of being with you. Kelly Ten Hagen and Lorrie Cummings, your friendship has been the source of support and happiness for decades. Thanks for never letting the conversation peter out. To my soul sister, Evelyn Roth, you have helped me endure the microstresses of everyday life for many years, and I could not be more grateful for the deep friendship we have built even while we live oceans apart. Donna Bowie, thanks for always making our lifelong friendship a priority. To my colleagues at Banyan, I consider myself fortunate indeed to work side by side with such a special group of people, particularly Meredith Nealon, with whom I relish the chance to meaningfully cocreate every day. Thank you for helping me to love my "day job" even more. To my friends and colleagues at Intermountain Healthcare Leadership Institute, especially Ilaria Cominotti, Travis Hansen, Julie Frahm, Angela Egner, Bruce Jensen, and Charles Sorenson, I appreciate your letting me explore and develop these ideas with you in real time. It's an honor to be part of your faculty, and even more to be your friend.

To our editors at Harvard Business Review, Susan Francis and Scott Berinato, I can't thank you enough for not only believing in this project but also bringing your A game to everything. You were the "dream team" of editors and I could not be more grateful. Jean Singer and Peter Gray, thanks for being such generous collaborators on this journey. Victoria Desmond and Patricia Boyd, thanks for making this book even better with your meticulous eyes. To our agent, Jim Levine, thanks for enthusiastically seeing the potential in this idea early on.

And finally, to my family, Richard, Rebecca, and Emma. Thank you for being the source of so much happiness in my life while still supporting my desire to continue to grow in new ways. Rebecca and Emma, as I watch you begin your own journey to find your place in this world, I could not be more proud of the rich, multidimensional lives you are building for yourselves. Thanks for making mine so much richer in the process, too.

—Karen Dillon

ABOUT THE AUTHORS

ROB CROSS has studied the underlying networks of effective organizations and the collaborative practices of high performers for more than twenty years. Working with more than three hundred organizations and reaching thousands of leaders from the front line to the C-suite, he has identified specific ways to cultivate vibrant, effective networks at all levels of an organization and any career stage. Through his research and writing, speaking and consulting, and courses and tools, Rob's network strategies are transforming how people lead, work, and live in a hyperconnected world.

Currently the Edward A. Madden Professor of Global Leadership at Babson College in Wellesley, Massachusetts, Rob is also the cofounder and director of the Connected Commons, a consortium of 150-plus leading organizations accelerating network research and practice.

He is the author of *Beyond Collaboration Overload* (Harvard Business Review Press, 2021), and has written more than fifty articles for *Harvard Business Review*, *Sloan Management Review*, *California Management Review*, and *Academy of Management Executive and Organizational Dynamics*. His work has been featured in venues such as *Businessweek*, *Fortune*, the *Financial Times*, *Time* magazine, the *Wall Street Journal*, *CIO*, *Inc.*, and *Fast Company*.

A graduate of the University of Virginia's McIntire School of Commerce (where he later taught), Rob earned an MBA from UVA's Darden School and completed doctoral work at Boston University. In his spare time, Rob has become an avid cyclist, logging 100 to 150 miles a week with a group of similarly foolish old guys. He also loves playing tennis, spending time on the water fishing and skiing, hiking, and listening to live music and is actively involved in his church. Practicing what he preaches on well-being, he recently became certified by the Professional Association of Diving Instructors for scuba and is loving the new world of friends and experiences that this aspect of life has opened up.

. . .

KAREN DILLON is a former editor of *Harvard Business Review* magazine and the coauthor of three books with Clayton Christensen: the *New York Times* bestseller *How Will You Measure Your Life?*, the *Wall Street Journal* business bestseller *Competing Against Luck: The Story of Innovation and Customer Choice*, and *The Prosperity Paradox: How Innovation Can Lift Nations Out of Poverty*. She is also the author of *The Harvard Business Review Guide to Office Politics*. A contributing editor to *Harvard Business Review* and editorial director of BanyanGlobal Family Business Advisors, Karen was named by Ashoka as one of the world's most influential and inspiring women.